HOW TO OVERCOME STRESS AND TENSION IN YOUR LIFE

HOW TO OVERCOME STRESS AND TENSION IN YOUR LIFE

TEDDY MOODY HEARD
and WYATT H. HEARD

Fleming H. Revell Company
Old Tappan, New Jersey

Scripture quotations are from the King James Version of the Bible.

Grateful acknowledgment is made to Charlotte Hale Allen for her editorial skills which contributed to the preparation of this volume, and to Dr. Irvin A. Kraft for the "ego structure" concept and diagram which formed the basis for Teddy Moody Heard's methodology.

Charts for "Developmental Tasks in Adulthood" were prepared by Sunday School Board of the Southern Baptist Convention. Used by permission.

Library of Congress Cataloging in Publication Data
Heard, Teddy Moody.
    How to overcome stress and tension in your life.

    1. Christian life—1960-   2. Stress (Psychology)
I. Heard, Wyatt H., joint author. II. Title.
BV4501.2.H369   248'.4   76-5850
ISBN 0-8007-0791-5

Lovingly dedicated to my grandfather,
George Harrison Moody, pioneer neurosurgeon
and psychiatrist in the state of Texas,
who spent his life demonstrating the principles
set forth in this volume;
and to my beautiful parents, Ted and Denman Moody,
who so faithfully shared them with me.

Teddy Moody Heard

Contents

Foreword

Stress is a condition which affects every twentieth-century man or woman. Doctors have long recognized the correlation between stress and diseases such as ulcers, high blood pressure, and drug addiction. Recently, however, we have become increasingly aware of the relationship between stress and heart disease, the chief cause of death in the United States. Since stressful situations are for the most part unavoidable, it is imperative that we learn to deal with them in a constructive, healthy manner. Too often, when confronted with an unpleasant task or decision, we tend to let it dominate our thoughts and actions without ever coming to grips with the problem. Fortunately it is possible for each of us to learn to face stress and tension in a thoughtful, rational manner and make the necessary mental and emotional adjustments. When properly channeled, stress can be beneficial as a tremendous source of energy and stimulation. Some lucky people seem to be born with the ability to handle stress effectively; others must learn to do so. Teddy and Wyatt Heard found a way that worked for them. For those who have ever felt stressed and nervous, and that includes most of us, this book should be helpful.

> Denton A. Cooley, M. D.
> Surgeon-in-Chief
> Texas Heart Institute

Prologue

There may be a few readers who are not aware of the special ways that God found to use Teddy Heard, and I'd like to share some of my own beautiful and rich experiences. This free, creative, wise, and fun-loving Christian—my dearest friend—had a profound influence on my own life. Let's go back to the pages of two of my own books—*Fishers of Men* and *Light My Candle.*

The title of this book [*Light My Candle*], with many of its concepts, anecdotes and illustrations, came from Teddy Heard, the very gifted and Spirit-filled wife of Judge Wyatt H. Heard of the 190th District Court of Texas.

There's no way to measure the effects of a Christian life such as Teddy's—a free, fun-filled, supereffective life—on other lives around her. . . .

Teddy, you see, is a fantastic Christian leader and one of the most vibrant and beautiful women I ever met. Sometimes you meet someone who is really on your wavelength, and when your friendship also is in the Lord, that makes the whole thing even more exciting. . . .

When you meet an exuberant, beautiful mother of four children who knows and loves the Lord, possesses great creative powers, enjoys a happy husband, a fantastic sense of humor and really abundant life—like our Teddy—you know you've discovered something rare. . . .

She literally had been fed God's Word from cradle days. Her parents taught her to seek answers to all life's problems in the Holy Bible. No wonder she had such wholeness, freedom, and a creative approach to life the rest of us envied but did not totally understand. . . .

Her calmness, clear thinking and wisdom of the Lord combined with a fantastic sense of fun—made problem-solving seem like a terrific adventure. . . .

When you'd share good news with Teddy, often she'd respond with some happy phrase from the Bible. She knew God's Word so well that a verse or so of lovely Scripture would spring to her lips as fast as a song might come to mine. . . .

She taught me so very much. It was hard to absorb it all—our experiences were so rich.

"One of the problems about trying to reach other people's deep feelings is, we're not in touch with our own deep feelings," Teddy said. "We tend to cushion ourselves against them, and we don't know what to do about them.

"We have to work through these, or else we won't have a testimony. . . .

"So many people have little dark rooms in their souls," Teddy said. "These rooms are buried deep—so deep within our will, intellect, or emotions that we keep them hidden even from ourselves. . . .

"When we allow the Spirit of God to shine in these dingy areas of our lives . . . Light heals these unhealthy places," she explained. "Jesus cleanses any diseased area of your life that you will yield to Him. . . . You are no longer dark in that area of your life. . . ."

Teddy Heard, more than any other person I ever knew, displayed the accepting, nonjudgmental, healing love of Jesus. Invariably people felt immediately drawn to her.

Teddy's kind of love—the love of Jesus—comes from God.

You will find here—in Teddy's own writing—a deep personal commitment to Christ. Through this book Teddy teaches us how to make an adventure of solving our problems and sharing our faith, and with the help of God and His Holy Word, I pray we will all learn how to overcome stress and tension in our lives.

ANITA BRYANT

I can do all things through Christ
which strengtheneth me.
Philippians 4:13

-1-

You've Got What It Takes

Each one of us has experienced the damaging effects of stress. Doctors say stress-sickness has become epidemic in our society. Every family suffers in some way from its effects: ulcers, drug dependency, obesity, premature heart attack or stroke, migraine headaches, arthritis, high blood pressure, acne, asthma, alcoholism, marital infidelity, suicide, and a dreary catalogue of similar complaints.

What is stress and what can we do about it?

Stress, a word borrowed from engineering and physics, literally means a force or system of forces sufficient to strain or deform a body. Stress "bends us out of shape." The dictionary traces the word to the Old French *estrece* which means narrowness, or the Latin *strictus* which means drawn tight. In other words: "in a bind"—"boxed in"—"in a pinch"—"a squeeze"—"a tight"—"uptight."

We understand those terms. We have all lived through times of such extreme need, fear, grief, or depression (and combinations of these) that mental and emotional paralysis sets in. Life situations sometime seem impossible to unravel. The ongoing stress which results can lead to despair, illness, or even a very real death of the spirit.

The Good News

The good news is—we've got what it takes to withstand pressures. The Bible tells us we can surmount anything life hands us. Yes, *anything.*

The answers may not be simple or what we think we want, but given time and a certain amount of practice, any of us can learn how to cope with stress.

Responding to stress is a learned experience. I *learn* stress responses just as I learn anything else. The process will involve attitudes, skills, and experiences. It will require longing, goal setting, failing sometimes, feeling inadequate, stretching new muscles, experiencing pain, and reaching goals.

Learning how to respond to stress involves learning how to maintain balance, and that requires practice. And *more* practice.

It is important to understand that the process of learning how to respond creatively to stress also becomes a way by which we can find ourselves—defining our greater strengths and lesser strengths to gain a clear perspective of *who we are* at this moment in time. For many of us an accurate and nonjudgmental look at the unique and interesting person we call "me" becomes a brand-new experience.

How Does Stress Help With All This?

We're accustomed to thinking of stress as something terrifying, ulcer making, and negative. Dr. Paul Tournier, the Swiss psychiatrist and author, argues on the other hand that stress has positive value as one of God's means whereby we can change and strengthen our lives. The Bible certainly bears out that idea. The Apostle Paul, for example, again and again demonstrates the principles of creative response to stress and how these principles work in every life situation.

But you say that you are not the Apostle Paul! True enough, but we cannot escape the fact that God has given us the same equipment, the same power, the same grace. As Paul wrote to the Ephesians: "For we are his workmanship, created in Christ Jesus unto good works, which God hath before ordained that we should walk in them" (2:10).

I like the way my friend John Wildenthal, Houston lawyer, civic leader, and prayer-group friend, puts it: "Stress is the pressure that produces growth." And I like the statement Dr. Arthur Hansen made when he was president of the Georgia Institute of Technology: "We don't teach our students to become engineers; we teach them to become problem solvers. Problem solving is the secret of life."

As we go along, we will discover indeed that problem solving can be learned. We will also learn how to use stress to create new strengths within us, instead of allowing it to continue to drain and weaken our lives. This may require some relearning. Unfortunately, many of us are so accustomed to living with worry, tension, abnormal guilt feelings, and other negative emotions that we accept them as a natural part of our environment.

Not so. We were created to be happy, productive,

and at ease in our world. It is *natural* for us to live this way because, whether or not we realize it, we were created with the tools, equipment, and design to handle any situation.

Individual Reactions to Stress

As I write these words, I yearn for you to know how much I identify with you. Essentially we share common feelings, experiences, triumphs, and tragedies. Your stress and my stress may be nearly identical at this moment or some other.

In this book, we will share many of these feelings and experiences. Since age seventeen I have investigated—conducted a really serious scientific study designed to find answers for the following questions:

- What is stress?
- How does stress affect individuals?
- Why do some people seem to take stress well while others go all to pieces?
- Is there a reason some persons respond well to incredibly large doses of stress, while others experience deep frustration when confronted with even small amounts?
- Are some people simply weak and unable to cope, while others are strong?
- Are the "weak ones" doomed to worry and ulcers, while others seem to suffer no permanent ill effects of real tragedy?

Obviously there are as many reactions to difficulty as there are individuals. There are sunny optimists, for example, whose cheerful words and smiling faces so often arouse hostility in those who are suffering.

Sometimes you hear people offer such words as "the joy of the Lord is your strength" to individuals literally ravaged with despair. You see the sufferer turn away from such evident lack of understanding and empathy, convinced he is dealing with a cold, uncaring person.

On the other hand, the individual who knows how to accept stress and gain dominion over circumstances possesses the kind of compassion (compassion means "feeling with") that heals. Acceptance, compassion, overcoming circumstances: Jesus came to teach us how to handle all these—and much, much more.

Learning to Cope

Most of my life I have studied questions concerning stress, human relationships, and man's psychological makeup. In the field of education in particular, I attempted to determine which developmental tasks form the foundation of a healthy, successful life.

During the years I taught elementary-age children I came to see that an individual's capacity for development results from opportunities for *specific learning,* rather than from acquiring some "perfect mechanism" with which to cope. In fact, there is no *perfect* mechanism.

Few of the principles we will discuss here are recent discoveries. Most grew out of my childhood training and represent the framework for responding to the realities of life as my parents presented them.

I watched my father utilize these basic concepts as he developed into a man of deep character, integrity, and devotion to family, as well as one of America's great trial lawyers, despite personal pressures that might have devastated others. My beautiful mother emerged, via these same life principles, as one of Houston's most beloved and respected women. She graciously and responsibly serves as God's person wherever she finds herself.

Happy is the child who discovers early that he can cope. One of the privileges of growing up with my parents was that they never tried to protect us from stress. When a problem—or even a crisis—arose they discussed the situation with us children.

Problems, even those which appeared too serious to permit a solution, were considered quite matter-of-factly. No one ever panicked. We children observed very early that problems did not control our parents, but our parents worked together and with us to find solutions for the difficult challenges of life.

The most inspiring examples of coping, however, cannot substitute for one's own experiences. In recent years, as the wife of a man in public life and the mother of four active children, and with my own schedule of family, personal, and community interests to maintain, I have been privileged to learn firsthand some creative responses to stress.

Stress Factors in Your Life

As you begin to consider your life, let me say that this book includes thoughts, methods, and suggestions which have been scientifically tested. Again and again, principles delineated here have proved to be observable, practical, demonstrable truths. These truths have worked for me. They have worked for hundreds of persons with whom I have shared insights regarding a wide spectrum of problems.

Like those others, you can learn how to make life more vital, joyous, and productive. You also can learn:

- How to live without fear and anxiety.
- How to handle pressures.
- How to concentrate on the needs of a given situation rather than your feelings of fear or helplessness.
- How to correctly appraise the situation from which your current stress or challenge arises.
- How to reevaluate your present goals and expectations.
- How to develop a plan of action.

As you respond to these fascinating challenges, you will discover new satisfactions in your increased personality skills. You will begin to interpret situations more realistically and increase the strengths you will need to handle them. Of course, this may include marshaling defenses so that you can live for a time even in *unresolved stress* without allowing it to dominate you.

Tools for Self-Research

As you begin researching your Self, you will want to keep two books close at hand. One is the Holy Bible, for every principle in this book can be backed up scripturally. Not only does the Bible provide colorful illustrations of every stress known to man, but it gives God's answers to each problem.

The texts and references used here will stand alone and do not require you to possess any special Bible knowledge. I will be using the King James Version. You may use any version you prefer.

You will also need a special notebook—a thick one—to record many of your experiments, experiences, and insights as we progress. It will make excellent reading a year from now: an honest and personal account of your unique struggles and successes. The title? Just for fun, why not call it *I've Got What It Takes*. That is exactly what we mean to prove.

-2-

You and I

Try saying this word aloud—"*I.*"

You just described your ego. Ego is your present consciousness of "I am." The word *ego*, I recently discovered, literally means "I"—a tiny word some of us do not adequately understand.

"When psychiatrists and psychologists use the word 'ego' it means something very different from ordinary usage," explained Dr. James D. Mallory, Jr., director of the Atlanta Counseling Center. "Many people use 'ego' to convey such ideas as selfish, puffed up, vain, better than others, or similar negative things.

"Ego, in the scientific sense, is a neutral word. It refers to that function of the mind that has awareness of self; that makes judgments; knows what I'm feeling, what I'm doing; that reaches out and assimilates facts, orders them, weighs them, and makes decisions based on sensory input."

Your "I Am" Feelings

For our purposes, therefore, *ego* means that rational, decision-making, evaluating, reasonable part of the brain which enables us to interpret correctly and respond appropriately to our life circumstances. Ego is that part of a person's special design and equipment which allows him to respond to life as *himself,* the truly precious and irreplaceable *I*.

In that context, let's experiment with ego—translated into the word *I*. To begin with, say it aloud once more—*I*.

How did that feel? Begin your notebook with a page that describes your I AM feelings. For example, you might write:

- I AM healthy.
- I AM punctual.
- I AM the oldest child in my family.
- I AM grumpy in the morning, but fun at night.

See what we are doing? In a not-too-serious way, we have begun to sketch in an idea portrait of that *I* of whom presently we may have only vague and hazy notions. Write as many I AMs as you can think of, then glance at the list. How many of your *I*s seem critical? Approving? Trivial? Honest? Positive or negative?

The list you just made may reveal some interesting new ego concepts, or it may not. What matters at this point, however, is that we begin to define that special set of traits, foibles, and distinguishing characteristics that allow us to respond to life as we do—the truly precious and irreplaceable *I*.

Healthy Ego

"Jesus Christ often described the acts of a healthy ego," Dr. Mallory said. "You will know the truth, and the truth will make you free" (*see* John 8:32)—"I am come that you might have life, and that more abundantly" (*see* John 10:10). Those are positive ego functions, Dr. Mallory explained.

The psychiatrist described the healthy ego as a person who has a reasonable assessment of who he is, who can correctly assess what is going on out there; who knows what reality is; who can make good judgments and reach conclusions about the true meanings of things—as opposed to one who is oversensitive or who overreacts. "It's a truism that a healthy person has a healthy ego," he concluded.

Keeping the healthy *I* in mind, let us explore a few working principles concerning ego. Let us agree, for example, that my ego identity is my present consciousness and awareness of who I am—how I perceive my environment and myself, and how I marshal my coping mechanisms.

Our goal? We want to build ego strength, and that depends greatly upon our finding the nourishment essential to the growth of our human potential. Ego strength also depends on our discovery of life sources into which we can plug our physical, emotional, and spiritual needs, satisfy those needs, and enable them to become mature and creative forces in and of themselves.

But I cannot develop faith in something—in this case,

my ego—until the concept becomes secured in my conscious mind. And only as we begin to appreciate our uniqueness, that one-of-a-kind Self, can we begin to fulfill God's will to become the special Self He envisions. *I believe the full realization of my potential is the ultimate fulfillment of His will.*

Ego Power and Self-Image

A minister tells a story about a four-year-old girl who invaded her father's study and hovered around until he stopped working and took her on his lap. "Honey, I want to tell you a secret," he said, and whispered into her ear, *"You are wonderful."*

"I have a secret for you, too, Daddy," she replied. He bent down to hear her whisper, "I know it!"

Egocentric? Vain? Self-satisfied? Of course not. But how many of us, when told we are wonderful, could say, "I know it?" Do you remember when you first caught a pure, sharp vision of your Self? When you realized you are *you?* That would be a good memory to record. Jot down exactly the self-image you had and how old you were at the time.

"I'm wonderful." Innocently and spontaneously the youngster reflects an accurate self-appraisal. She really is wonderful, as we all are. The Bible calls us children of God, created a little lower than the angels, able to do all things through Christ.

We are wonderful! The little girl, thankfully, still is free to think so and say so, because society has not yet taught her that it is not "nice" to appreciate herself.

She has what I call *ego power.* A person who is "stuck

together on the inside with plenty of love," as my daughter Susanna once described it, possesses ego power. The person who takes time out occasionally to assess himself, his values, his position on things—the individual who attempts to get a sharp and honest focus on himself—strengthens his ego power.

A female advertising executive takes time once a year to write her personal credo. This sort of action, or anything else that helps us know our Selves, definitely helps us increase our ego power. This power enables us to function as reasonable and capable personalities. It enables us to make decisions, and to make them sensibly.

You Are What You Decide

A popular magazine featured a test by which readers could measure their abilities to make decisions. The article described good decision making as central to a healthy personality and a successful life. Accordingly, let us examine a life principle upon which *all behavior* is based.

- My actions and my responses are based on decisions I make.
- The success of my decision making directly relates to:

    1. My ability to correctly perceive my environment requirements, or accurately perceive the situation in which I find myself.

    2. My ability to adequately appraise my greater and lesser strengths and my ability to use them

to cope with my perception of my environment.

You are a decision maker. Every day you make doz-
ens of decisions, ranging from what to order for break-
fast to the choice of college, career, or marriage mate.
Your ego dictates these choices and decisions, based on
a number of factors:

- Accumulation of necessary information.
- The way you feel about yourself.
- How often you allow other persons to control you,
  to make your conscious or unconscious decisions
  for you.
- How flexible you are in reevaluating old goals and
  expectations and setting new ones.
- How adept you are in marshaling coping mechanisms when you are required to respond to a
  person or situation.
- How consistent you are in seeking God's guidance.
- How willing you are to make necessary changes.

Good decision making helps us develop ego muscle.
Later in this book we will discuss some methods of
strengthening our abilities for decision. Meanwhile you
might start a new workbook page entitled DECISIONS
and list those which presently stare you in the face.
Write these out concisely and place today's date beside
them.

Later we will tackle these decisions to be made, and
apply some potential ego power to the situation. Re-

member that the principles outlined in this book apply to anyone who makes decisions, anyone who encounters problems, and anyone who experiences stress. That means *each of us.*

Sound Decision Making

My father's verbal, *commonsense* instructions and my mother's verbal, *scriptural* instructions taught me very early that there are sound ways to make decisions —and that those who refuse to decide, nevertheless *are deciding* to do nothing.

When I was sixteen, a pretty schoolmate asked if she could come home with me after school and talk. She was a vivacious girl who started dating earlier than most, and the boys joked about what a good time anyone had if they took her out.

In my room she closed the door, sat on the bed, and began to weep. At last she confessed that she had slept with a boy and was afraid she was pregnant. "I have ruined my life," she sobbed. "I don't want to be that kind of person. I know I have a bad reputation, and I'm not only scared, but I'm sick about myself. I tried to think how I can change and suddenly I thought about you. It took a lot of courage, but I knew I wanted to tell you and see if you have any ideas."

During her confession I asked myself: "Why don't *I* sleep with boys?" Slowly I began to remember how my decision had come about, and told my friend:

"Two years ago Mama told me boys would want to express affection in different ways, and it was important for me to think about the ways I think are okay and those I don't think are okay. She told me three places I could go for information to back up my decision." (I remember my amazement at the intent way my friend listened to every word.)

"First, Mother reminded me of what we always do when there is an important decision to be made: look in the Bible and find out what God says on the subject. Second, she recommended that I read a book on teenage dating to discover good psychological guidelines for setting values and standards in expressing love before marriage. Then I was to consult my own Self, knowing I want to be God's person and grow into happy, free adulthood."

I described to my friend how Mama gave me an assignment: I was to write down all the verses I could find in the biblical concordance under *love, adultery, fornication,* and so on. Then I read a book about dating that made good sense to me, putting in modern language many of the same things I had read in the Bible.

Several days later Mother and I talked more about the subject. I showed her everything I had written down from both books and how alike they were. She explained again that God tells us truths about human nature as well as Himself, and that if we let Him guide us we may go in a different direction than if we pay no attention to Him.

Mother asked me to divide my new knowledge into two columns listing: FACTS ABOUT HEAVY SEX BEFORE MARRIAGE and FACTS ABOUT WAITING FOR HEAVY SEX UNTIL AFTER MARRIAGE. She asked me to put my conclusions and my decision into writing after I completed the lists.

"Well, quick, tell me what happened and what did you decide?" my friend asked.

"There was no doubt about what I wanted to do," I told her. "I just looked at those two lists and knew which one was for me."

"Teddy, you are so lucky you have a mother who showed you how to do all that," she said.

My friend also learned how to make deliberate and rational decisions instead of living by impulse. The first and most important decision she made was to invite Christ into her heart.

Later, she and I were able to rehearse ways for her to explain to boys that her life was different from the days in which she had courted so freely. She learned to say something like, "This may be hard for you to understand. I like you as my friend, but I've changed my mind about how I want to show friendship for you. That other way was not good for me. We can still be friends and go out if you are willing to let me show friendship for you in some new ways."

Some of the boys made fun of her and said, "That won't last long," but she began developing a new circle of friends. She started attending church and later joined. She learned how to receive genuine love, develop her talents, and share her faith. Now she is a radiant Christian mother married to one of our city's most successful Christian businessmen.

Today my friend's most wonderful gift is her deep sensitivity to young girls who have not had the benefit of a home in which they are taught sound, life-producing thought patterns. God has used her numerous times to help youngsters take an accurate reading of the truth, reevaluate personal goals, and devise a new plan of action. (*See* Chapter 9, "Creative Response to Stress," for more examples of the Key—a valuable tool in stress situations.)

She had a profound influence on my life, too. I shall never forget the helpless look on her face when she said I was so fortunate to have someone to teach me how to live. At that moment I realized the responsibility of sharing with others any good thing that someone else shares with us.

It's Never Too Late

Whether we are sixteen or sixty-one, it is important to remember that we *learn* to respond to decisions, problems, and stresses. These skills do not just come naturally, but must be acquired. Some people seem to respond to problems with very little anxiety, while others feel swamped most of the time. Some individuals may find they only occasionally overreact to stress, but would like to become more in control. Still others who occupy helping roles will want to know how to share ways to guide others in building healthy ego muscle.

Whatever your position at this time, I believe the principles outlined here can revolutionize your life. Moreover, our journey of self-discovery and ego identity will prove again and again an astonishingly powerful truth: *Our greatest growth comes from stress.*

We do not understand the magnificent love of God until—in stress situations—we give Him an opportunity to reveal Himself to us. As we were growing up, however, some of us learned these ineffective stress responses:

- Don't worry. Things will get better.
- Ignore it and it will go away.
- It's really not that bad.
- Peace at any cost.

We desperately need new orientation to the reality of stress in our lives, and to the total adequacy of our potential ability to cope in the midst of it. For this we must seek a *questing* creativity, a *healing* creativity. But first we need to find and recognize the real *I*, the pure ego, the untarnished Self.

Ego is beautiful. In order to discover the God-given *I*, however, we must return to the original design. Each of us needs to find his own divine blueprint, brush off the dust, and take a fresh look at His plan.

Only one life in Creation will have your name on it.

-3-

Your Blueprint

From the initial instant of your conception, you and your life originated from a unique blueprint which never will be copied.

What extravagant planning! Can you imagine any human builder so wasteful as to insist on unimpeachable individuality within every unit he will ever construct? "An acorn inevitably must grow into an oak tree," someone said, "and just as certainly, each of us is destined to develop according to divine plan."

What is my inner design? My internal plan? Where is the blueprint of my life? How do I find it? How can I build from it the sound, actualized structure which God intends my life to reveal?

The Bible instructs us to seek the Kingdom of God (*see* Matthew 6:33). The Word also says: "The Kingdom of God is within you" (*see* Luke 17:21). Can it be, then, that in order to find the Kingdom we first must seek out our Selves?

How do we go about finding the authentic blueprint? I believe that as surely as each individual possesses a unique destiny, it remains equally true that each has a unique capacity to build a sound, divinely joined and fitted ego structure.

Learning to Construct

Few of us seem naturally blessed at orderly construction methods. We manage to complete a few airy, pleasant rooms at the cost of leaving off others entirely. In some places the foundation of our lives seems shaky. Here and there the roof leaks. Piles of unused lumber, embarrassingly mixed with trash and rubbish, litter the outskirts of our construction sites. Why is this?

Tragically few of us do-it-yourselfers ever attempt to discover the original plan for our identity. It requires a search, after all, often a troublesome and painful search. Instead of seeking our Selves—seeking the Kingdom—it seems we prefer to let others tell us who we are. We permit our environments to delineate the boundaries of our lives, thus inhibiting the full development which God intended our inner man to experience.

How do we turn this process around? In order to become a fully self-actualized person, capable of responding creatively to environment, rather than being controlled by it, we must search diligently for glimpses of our original blueprint's intent. We must learn ways to build a strong, well-integrated structure from within. Our human potential offers us the equipment, the capacity, but not the power to generate our design's total actualization.

A primary goal for successful living should be *to be-*

come involved in an ongoing learning process, thus enabling your potential to become actualized.

The One and Only You

Are you truly convinced that you are special? Original? Unique? Never to be duplicated? Some days we feel certain that we possess no special qualities whatever. If you feel that way now, it is important to isolate those traits or qualities which distinguish you: looks, skills, intellectual capacities, and so on.

At this juncture you might list MY SPECIAL TRAITS and itemize those certain distinguishing things you enjoy about yourself: blue eyes, talent for music, good sense of humor, good tennis game, personal warmth, and so on—all that combines to make up the package labeled YOU. Even the sketchiest list cannot help but convince you that each of us remains impossible to duplicate. At the same time the Bible says that within each one it *is* possible to find the Kingdom of God!

That one fact of Creation alone staggers the imagination. Accordingly, today I yearn to challenge you to the very depths of your being. I long to see you begin to seek out your own ignored or undiscovered blueprint, bring it into the daylight, and begin to read the Lord's plans for your life.

Help us remember, dear God, that where we will allow You into our lives, there do You become creative! Help us realize that we have let ourselves become so dominated and inhibited by the boundaries of habit and other people's expectations that we cease to see the undeveloped, unexplored territory still existing within.

We have listened to other voices and other circumstances for so long that we have become misinformed about our Selves. We are dulled from the effects of repeated incorrect or impotent information. We have lost contact with our Selves and with You.

Now look at your list entitled MY SPECIAL TRAITS. Compare that workbook page to the one entitled I AM. What do you see? Has the blueprint begun to emerge?

Emotional Maturity

The motivational energy of God's life is the power of actualization. Giving up one's will and saying *yes* to new possibilities opens the floodgate of His power. What some psychologists call *self-actualization* well might be compared to the late Dr. William C. Menninger's criteria for determining emotional maturity:

- The ability to deal constructively with reality.
- The capacity to adapt to change.
- Relative freedom from symptoms produced by tensions and anxieties.
- The capacity to find more satisfaction in giving than in receiving.
- The capacity to relate to other people in a consistent manner with mutual satisfaction and helpfulness.
- The capacity to sublimate, to direct one's instinctive hostile energy into creative and constructive outlets.
- The capacity to love.

Where do we find authoritative guidelines toward that sort of emotional maturity? Not surprisingly, you will find these principles demonstrated in the teachings of Jesus. It was Jesus, after all, who promised that the Kingdom of God is within us.

A Balanced Life in an Uneven World

Jesus ministered—and ministers today—to every aspect of man: mind, body, and spirit. Through His example and His teachings, we understand that God created man as a balanced, triune being.

Do you live a lopsided life? Most of us do. Perhaps we emphasize the intellect, value our spiritual nature, and meanwhile live in a flabby, ill-kept, run-down body. Of course, overemphasis on any one aspect of man's created nature will result in imbalance. It just won't work. Body, mind, and spirit—God obviously intends for all three parts to function in harmonious health together.

Seek ye first your own blueprint for life. Interestingly enough, those who attempt to seek God's divine plan for them invariably begin to experience a new balance, an unprecedented emotional stability as a result.

I thank God I am coming to a new understanding of Him as not dictating to me from the sky or from the pages of a book, but rather as actualizing His image through my life, through the very design of my being. As I am able to *become* my design and reflect an accurate picture of God's creative love, so will I, in union with His vitality, experience abundant life and share it with others.

My great interest now is to find the Life Sources necessary to actualize my design. This excites me beyond the power of words to express. I yearn to convey this excitement to you. I yearn to know you, because you are unique and irreplaceable. Furthermore, God cares about your going out and coming in; the very hairs of your head are numbered; you literally are precious to Him, for He bought you with a terrible price (*see* Proverbs 5:21; Matthew 10:30; 1 Corinthians 6:20).

Well might we ask ourselves, "Oh, God, who am I? Who have You designed?," for He hears our questions. The Bible says: "Ask and ye shall receive" (*see* Matthew 7:7, 8). God wants to reveal each man's special blueprint through the unfolding of his life.

-4-

Recognizing Our Ego Holes

All stress in one way or another threatens my identity —my "I am" feelings. On a certain day a man's secretary phones in sick; his driver smashes the company truck; he hunts all morning for an important, misplaced file. Then a client phones to denounce him for late delivery of needed goods and cancels the order, calling him "small-time and incompetent."

At that point the businessman may agree. Stress has overwhelmed his feelings about himself and his ability to deliver the goods. He feels angry, frustrated, helpless, and put down. "I'm no businessman. Everything's going down the drain," he tells himself.

Is the assessment correct? Probably not. Most likely the broad assault of stresses has exposed his "ego holes" (*see* Chapter 8) and allowed all sorts of subconscious fears, hostilities, anxiety, and low self-esteem to pour out. His thinking becomes confused, his reactions uncertain, his ability to "take it" begins to fray.

We have all had experiences like that. Denman, our young son, spills a glass of milk just as a long-distance phone call comes in. Someone accidentally lets the dog out and she bounds into the street. By the time I have completed the phone call, milk has run down the table leg and made a puddle on the floor, and as I mop it up, the doorbell rings.

"I'm a rotten housekeeper!" I say, as all sorts of negative feelings surface through one of my main ego holes —my doubt as to whether I will *ever* become an excellent housekeeper.

What are ego holes, anyhow? They are those weak or undeveloped areas that every life contains: the thing in me that "I just can't do anything about," the skills that "I never learned to do" or that "I don't want to do," the experiences other people know about and I choose to avoid.

Dealing With Ego Holes

Even if we know we have ego holes, too few of us choose to recognize them. As we mature chronologically we become adept at skirting the various potholes in our construction sites. Nevertheless, when a dark and stormy hour occurs, the holes are still there. We can trip and take a bad spill because of them.

There are two ways we can look at an ego hole. We can consider it a weakness or a blank spot in our makeup—or we can consider it as unrealized potential, that part of our design which remains to be explored and increased.

The moment we recognize our clear choice between these alternatives is the time we begin to assume control over our life's direction. To recognize and define our ego holes allows us to put boundaries on our vague, usually incorrectly expressed anxieties. We can pin down the source of much of our stress. We can discover a basis for correcting false self-information, and a reasonable base from which to proceed with decisions.

You Can Grow as Far as You Can Perceive

Do you perceive yourself correctly? Suppose you asked each member of your family to write a one-page profile about you, describing your personality and its main strong and weak traits. Meanwhile, suppose you wrote a similar paper about yourself.

When you read all the honest (though incomplete) sketches of the Self you are, what do you suppose would emerge? Would all the descriptions agree? Would you see yourself as others see you? Do you even recognize the person they describe?

"There are two kinds of honesty," one man says. "There's the honesty between my neighbor and me, and there's the honesty between me and me. I'm the only person in the world who can be responsible for knowing myself and not lying to myself."

One of the most valuable self-discoveries we can make deals with our individual ego holes. As we begin to admit them, disclose them to ourselves, probe them for their origins and their power to rule over our present lives, we often come into startling new knowledge about ourselves.

I shall never forget my surprise the day Jerry Bryant, our dear friend from San Antonio, told about one of his ego holes. Jerry is vice-president of the Frost National Bank, a highly successful man from any standpoint, and a loving and sensitive Christian. Imagine the incongruity of learning that a man like Jerry feels, in his words, "stupid, a real dodo, where sports are concerned."

Nor is that unimportant. Jerry explained that, in a man's world, knowing and caring about football or basketball scores, guiding and taking an interest in one's sons' development in sports is a big deal. Jerry told me about growing up unable to participate in team sports and convincing himself that it didn't matter. From there he went on to persuade himself that he "hated" organized games, and made a point of not bothering to know anything concerning sports.

Jerry thought his ego hole would cover over once he graduated from school. It was easy enough for him to skirt the athletics issue as a young man breaking into the business world, but during those years his self-opinion in that one area began to weaken. Eventually he had to admit to himself that his resistance to sports topics robbed him of relating to co-workers and other friends, male and female, in that one area of life. It robbed him conversationally, recreationally, and experientially.

Is this any big deal? When he reached his forties, Jerry began to admit to himself that it was. He disliked the limits he had placed on himself and disliked the low self-esteem which that particular ego hole was promoting. He took a good look at the situation and decided:

- Since he never would play pro football or baseball, his lack of size and weight are not important.

- Lack of experience and known skills need not hinder him from taking up handball, tennis, or golf.
- Nobody else knows or cares how well he might play.
- He could learn to enjoy sports via television, newspaper and magazine articles, and conversation with other fans.
- He wanted to rid himself of the negative feelings that ego hole had produced over a period of many years.

Jerry expressed gratitude for the decision he had made. He recognized that it represented a step forward in his personal development, a perfecting of God's blueprint. It might seem an insignificant decision in the eyes of some, but Jerry very wisely knows that God does not want our lives filled with hindrances, impediments, and what the Bible calls stumbling blocks. Jesus calls us to abundant life.

Recognizing our ego holes and describing them accurately and nonjudgmentally is an important first step toward a new ability to deal creatively with our stresses.

Is Your Ego Hole Your Identity?

Most stress *is* a stress because it threatens one's identity, your concept of yourself as a person. Who are you at the moment the milk puddles on the kitchen floor? You may see yourself—incorrectly—as a "rotten housekeeper," and that concept increases your feelings of stress.

Dr. Anthony M. Kowalski of the Menninger Foundation in Topeka, Kansas, elaborated on that idea in a letter he wrote to me:

> When I mulled over the concept of "ego holes," another thought occurred to me in addition to the one you expressed. One of the difficulties with such deficiencies, at least in my clinical experience, has been that these weaknesses extend and overlap into a number of different areas of functioning. If a person has an inadequate sense of being lovable, this may extend into his perception of his work or even sometimes physical functioning. One example that comes to me is that of a woman who perceived her femininity as meaning that she was somehow a second class citizen. This attitude overlapped into her style of thinking so that she felt her thoughts and ideas were second class and constantly not worth sharing with others, and you can guess the consequences. . . .

The ego hole, of course, is *not* your identity. It is important to realize that a "rotten housekeeper" or "second-rate businessman" or "unskilled sportsman" is *not* who you are. Every one of these negative summations, these ego holes, threatens our identity and creates new stress in us.

Creative Use of Ego Holes

What stress really does is signal us—*identify yourself!* It is the red flag waving at one's personal construction site: "Danger"—"Watch your step"—"Weak or temporary footing ahead."

When you know your identity you can properly respond to any stress by thought, word, and action. If you do not know your identity, you need to begin the search. Tragically few of us are taught how to make such an examination. Most of us do not go to the trouble or pain to discover our identities, but go through life allowing others to tell us who we are.

Delineating personal ego holes becomes an invaluable first step in seeking a correct picture of one's ego or identity. Using your workbook, begin a new page entitled EGO HOLES. As weak or incomplete areas of your life come to mind, list them here. You may not think of anything at all today, or you may quickly jot down a dozen.

One friend told me she could just write "everything" because everything bothered her. Indeed her list did become extensive as she noted such things as "fear of skiing"—"refusal to travel"—"not liking to talk to strangers."

Today this woman credits the list making with beginning her "turnaround," and the numbers of ego holes which she found so threatening and painful to disclose even to herself have been dealt with *only* because she honestly confronted herself with them.

Honesty, in this and all other exercises in this book, remains of first importance. Our Lord said, "And ye shall know the truth, and the truth shall make you free" (John 8:32). Therefore we call to our minds whatever ego holes make us stumble along the way, thanking Him for the faith and the knowledge that healing is possible. *Those holes are not your identity.*

A Nonjudgmental Spirit

It is important to view our ego holes as interesting phenomena in our existences, rather than any measure of our success or failure in life. *Therefore we will not judge or blame ourselves or others for negative spots in our structures.* This is not to be a faultfinding session, but an hour when it is time to turn God's light on the dark rooms in our lives.

With this attitude firmly fixed, we now want to seek God's wisdom as to where and when a particular ego hole originated. Sometimes we can fix on the situation where it began, as in the case of the businessman whose late delivery of goods cost him a customer. "It began when I was a boy," he said. "My parents were standing on the back porch, calling me for supper. As I walked toward them I could hear my father muttering to himself, 'That kid's never going to amount to much.' That attitude persisted until the day he died. I realize how much of my life I've spent trying to prove him wrong."

That is the sort of insight God can provide when we allow him to show us, objectively and kindly, both the ego hole and its source.

Obviously, the businessman—once the root cause of his stress was uncovered—might have run the danger of hating his father, blaming his parents for his troubles, or accepting his father's evaluation of him. None of these reactions would help him, of course.

What we need most of all is an accurate view of our ego holes as they exist today, with some insight, where possible, into their genesis. What we do *not* need is a spirit of faultfinding, blame placing, or sense of "What's the use!" We need to agree with ourselves right now that if we discover any tendencies towards self-disparagement or self-hatred we will weed them out immediately. These have no place in the garden that surrounds God's construction site.

Dealing With an Ego Hole

Here's one example, as Caroline told it:

> I was forty-five years old before I could admit feelings of shame and inadequacy over something really very silly. You'll think I'm terribly dumb, but through all those years of school and marriage and working and child rearing, I never drove a car. We always managed to find some way around it because I really didn't want to drive.
>
> Then we moved to the suburbs. Don couldn't spend all his time taking me places and the children weren't home much anymore. I was stranded. Everyone in the family tried to persuade me to take driving lessons and buy a car, and I knew they were right.
>
> But even I had no idea how big an ego hole the nondriving thing had become. I tried to talk myself into the right attitude, prayed about it, gave myself little pep talks—everything. I did such a good job on myself that soon I really anticipated that first driving lesson.
>
> About thirty minutes before the driving instructor arrived, however, I sort of fizzled inside. I couldn't believe the turmoil I felt, or the tightness in my throat. I scolded myself mentally, called myself neurotic, and reminded myself that everybody else drives cars, even

dull-witted people and people with real physical handicaps. There was absolutely no reason on earth why I should excuse myself from learning such an ordinary task.

The pep talk didn't work. I felt paralyzed and helpless. I simply couldn't figure out this fear. In fact, it wasn't really fear at all, but some other feeling I couldn't define, a powerful feeling that was convincing me it would be downright dangerous for me to drive a car.

In desperation, I began to pray. I asked God to show me exactly where such an irrational feeling came from. His answer came instantly, so absolutely right and compelling that I felt like shouting!

As soon as the prayer left my lips, a picture formed in my mind: a small girl astride a tricycle with high wheels, riding her trike down steep stairs to show off to her small friends.

Other pictures followed: climbing high into towering trees; walking barefoot along a picket fence to prove I wasn't scared to do it; making a "parachute jump" off the garage roof with my mother's umbrella.

Then came the most telling picture of all—that of my parents denying me roller skates or a bicycle because I'd probably break my neck, and guilty memories of sneaking around the corner and learning how, anyway. Those guilt memories and that pain had been buried and forgotten for more than thirty years. It amazed me to see how *strong* those feelings were when they returned!

Caroline's ego hole and its beginnings, once revealed, did not magically go away. She still has strong inhibitions about driving, but she understands where they originated and knows they are not valid for her life today. She laughed as she continued:

> Those pictures the Lord showed me proved I came out of my harum-scarum childhood with my neck miraculously intact, but a head full of misinformation. I saw that I perceived myself, subconsciously, as a dangerous daredevil: someone you wouldn't trust with wheels, and worst of all, someone who cheated her parents and *wanted wheels, anyhow.* No wonder I've lived all these years refusing to give myself a car!

Did Caroline blame her parents for their seeming overprotectiveness? "Not a bit," she said. "My shenanigans must have driven them almost crazy. I'm sure they felt it was absolutely necessary to 'ground me' as much as possible."

Caroline further realized that *her parents* never called her irresponsible, dangerous, or unfit to operate an automobile. She had made that judgment *herself*, based on their early refusal of bicycling and skating privileges. Since the judgment took place entirely on a subconscious level, she had no way to rebut it. Caroline told me:

> If I had not confronted myself with that ego hole and asked God to explain it to me, I feel sure I might have struggled against my inhibition forever.

Not always will we receive the clear-cut knowledge that allows us to understand where our main ego holes began. But until we are willing to acknowledge at least the presence of a weakness, to view it without judgment or blame, and to seek to understand the frailty, it will remain intact—a hole through which fear, anxiety, and confusion can erupt anytime stress appears.

-5-

Developmental Tasks

"All life is a process, and for a process to continue, there must be change," Dr. Karl Menninger wrote in *The Vital Balance*. There are certain timetables for learning, and when a task is improperly learned or left out altogether, this creates an ego hole.

For example, if a grammar-school child does not learn to read, the ego hole now developing can distort his self-image far into the future: "I am dumb"—"Reading isn't fun for me"—"I'm not smart enough to go to college." Later in life he may describe his spouse and children as much brighter than he—people who "read all the time."

Most of us try to compensate for that sort of ego hole, to cover it up or pretend it does not exist, though we are conscious that the weak spots remain beneath the floor of our lives. It takes real energy to continue remembering to avoid them, to step carefully so we do not fall into a dark basement filled with feelings of insecurity and dissatisfaction.

The ideal answer, of course, is to learn life's lessons decently and in order at the times when society or our own personalities require. When a child approaches school age his mother wants to send him to first grade equipped to hold his own with other children. During the months prior to the big day she makes sure he knows his name and address, knows how to dress himself and tie his shoes, understands about riding the school bus, can cross a street safely, and other tasks appropriate to his age and circumstances.

Proper acquisition of skills establishes strong, healthy ego muscle, of course. Every job we do well increases our confidence, our joy, our good sense of "I am." Conversely, as we learned earlier, the unlearned skill or the incorrectly learned skill will trip us up just about every time or at least may distort our life unnecessarily, as in the case of Caroline, who all those years had to have her husband, neighbor, or teenager drive her to the grocery store.

What about developmental tasks? Later in this chapter I am going to list groups of adult skills we should be working on or have already mastered within specific periods of our adult lives. It is too late, of course, to do much about undeveloped skills of childhood. *Or is it?* More about that later, too.

The Skills We Skipped

Ask any roomful of adults about childhood developmental tasks they missed or skipped, and you get some pretty funny answers. "The only reason I know right from left," a minister told me, "is that I remember as a tot that when I sucked my thumb it always was the left one. That's the only way I can remember *left* and *right* to this day."

"I never learned the alphabet," a woman confessed. "Since I could read when I started school, they put me in the second grade. You learn the alphabet in the first grade, and I was ashamed to tell anyone I didn't know it. In fifth grade I was horrified to discover we were going to have to learn to put words in alphabetical order. I panicked because I couldn't think of any way to fake it. A timely case of mumps saved me from the ordeal of being exposed as someone who didn't know the alphabet. By the time I returned to school my teacher excused me from making up the work because she thought I read so well that she felt certain I surely knew how to alphabetize!"

The above two examples probably sound trivial and ludicrous, but they point out one thing. All of us "stayed in bed with mumps" when something important came along, and all of us experienced ego holes from unlearned developmental tasks.

The lady who never learned the alphabet hardly suffers at all, except when she needs to look up a telephone number. But if her job required her to know the alphabet—if she were a file clerk, for example, or a librarian—she would develop stress! Likewise, we might imagine the clergyman as an army private, mentally popping his thumb in his mouth before he could obey orders to turn to the left or to the right.

A ridiculous image? Almost any one of us could reveal something equally silly about ourselves, if ego holes could talk—as of course, in a way, they really do.

The Value of Developmental Tasks

Assuming you took things as they came during most of your childhood, you may have found yourself entering adulthood with good feelings about yourself and your abilities, and able to make strong and right decisions when you need to.

Without such experiences, however, ego holes may release floods of doubt and indecision, feelings of helplessness and inadequacy, because you do not know from experience what you *may* do in a certain situation, or what you *should* do. No wonder the Bible says: "Train up a child in the way he should go: and when he is old, he will not depart from it" (Proverbs 22:6).

Parents quickly discover that one of their most difficult and important jobs is to maintain some perception of their growing child's ever-changing ego capacity. Problems arise if children are brought into the larger world before they learn those tasks necessary to fit them for that world. A child's ego capacity (and ours, too) depends upon how well he has learned to perceive reality, and how successful he has become in marshaling coping mechanisms, his major strengths, to deal with life situations.

It should go without saying that even though a teenager has learned his middle-childhood tasks very well, it is impossible to expect him to thrive in an adult world which requires ego strength based only on having learned developmental tasks of the adolescent. It should go without saying, yes—but how often do we see supposedly intelligent parents allow or even push their children into situations they are not prepared to experience: parties where there is drinking, perhaps, or lack of chaperonage!

In training our children, there are excellent books to help alert us to some of the main learning skills necessary at various stages of life. The best book for teaching developmental tasks, however, will always be the Bible. Parents who regularly read the Book of Proverbs, for example, are filling their minds with facts about what God wants us to be. We can and we should, from the very outset, train up those children—train ourselves, too—as He instructs us.

Identity Crisis

Teddy, our older daughter, as early as age two possessed a deep, strong, remarkable singing voice. All her life she has had an adult-sounding voice—rich and throaty—and long before she started school our friends would ask Teddy to sing for them. She enjoyed singing and we encouraged her to do so.

One day when she was eight she came home from school, sobbing as though her heart would break. She was crying so hard that at first she couldn't tell me what was wrong, but at last the story came out. Her teacher had asked her to sing "America" and she obeyed the request. All the other children laughed at her, wouldn't stop laughing, and she would "never, never sing again."

I hardly knew what to say, especially since I sensed that for little Teddy this would be a moment of destiny. I sent a silent little SOS to God and began to talk to my daughter, holding her in my arms as she trembled and sobbed. Gently I explained that she had a deep voice that sounded more like a grown person than a child, and the other children probably thought that was funny. It would be easy to see how they might feel like laughing, but their laughter made her feel . . . (and here I paused).

"Terrible, Mama!" she burst out. "I just can't stand it!" she wept. I felt like weeping, too, as—feeling my way along very carefully—I talked about how God creates us all different, how the Bible says we each have different gifts, and how we knew that one of her special gifts was an unusual voice.

"Remembering that God made you this way, gave you this particular voice, and entrusted you with a gift, would you like to just ask Him what He would like you to do about this?" I suggested.

Instantly she slid off my lap and we knelt beside my bed. (This makes tears come to my eyes as I remember it.) She poured out her little heart to God, told Him everything she felt, adding that she just didn't ever want to encounter such laughter again. Then she told God she knew that He had created her, had even put her in our family, and that He had given her a gift for singing. Still weeping, she gave that gift right back to Him and gave herself to Him, and I wept, too. It was a precious moment.

I wish I could say that Teddy never had another problem, but that is not true. From time to time she would be asked to sing, and children usually laughed at her. Her decision had been made that day on her knees, however, and she never wavered from it. "They all laughed, but Mama, I know who I am," she would say.

"I am God's person and He gave me my voice."

Little Teddy set me a good example that day. She showed me once again that establishing one's identity is always painful, that it always costs. That child has been an inspiration to me. She has a freedom of spirit that comes from knowing she is God's person.

For each one of us, problems will arise when we come out into the world before we have learned those tasks necessary for living in the world. Teddy's problem was unique to her, perhaps, in her eight-year-old environment. Today she remembers that stress as one that strengthened her, that made her even more aware of her special "I am." Had she not dealt with the situation the very day it occurred, however, she might very well have developed instead an ego hole labeled "voice" or "ridicule" or "other people's opinions," or some such thing.

There's a specific time to learn each developmental task, and very often the best time is the day the need arises.

Developmental Tasks in Adulthood

One of my husband's favorite documents, which he uses consistently in adult teaching, lists developmental tasks we should accomplish as young adults, median adults, and senior adults. Wyatt considers this chart (prepared by Adult Section, Baptist Sunday School Board) a wonderful yardstick. We will use it to measure ourselves now.

We are going to consider developmental tasks within eight different areas of life according to our present stage of adulthood. It's also interesting to look at any earlier stage or stages to make sure that we have learned those tasks previously.

When you encounter a developmental task you consider improperly learned or not yet learned, note this on a workbook page entitled EGO HOLES. Later you will want to consider these items in detail and make some decisions regarding them.

With faithful pen and notebook at hand, let us begin by considering each stage of our development as adults.

YOUNG ADULTS

Family

Choosing a mate and/or adjusting to unmarried adult status

Learning to live in the marriage relationship

Setting up standards and values for the home

Adjusting to children in the family

Training and nurturing small children

Adjusting to and preparing children for school

Growing in the ability to manage a home

Vocational

Choosing and getting started in an occupation

Striving for status in the occupation

Improving in occupational efficiency

Physical	Establishing wholesome standards for physical health
	Controlling and directing sexual drives
Social	Finding a congenial social group
	Participating in constructive leisure-time activities
	Achieving socially responsible behavior
	Adopting motives and standards for social relationships
Economic	Achieving economic independence from parents
	Living within the income
	Facing frequent necessity of working wife/mother
	Anticipating educational expense for children
Civic	Accepting responsibility as a citizen
	Developing concepts and skills necessary for civic competence
Spiritual Growth	Experiencing or evaluating conversion
	Developing a Christian philosophy of life
	Establishing significant worship patterns
	Growing in use of the Bible as a guidebook
	Increasing in ability to witness to one's faith

Growing in understanding of theological truth

Church Relation   Establishing a meaningful church relationship

Continuing one's preparation for service in the church

Accepting increasingly significant roles in church

Developing in service potential

MEDIAN ADULTS

Family   Guiding family relations in the home

Assisting teenage children to become responsible persons

Reinforcing standards and values for the home

Discovering satisfying relationships with aging parents

Readjusting to spouse as children leave home

Relating to grandchildren

Vocational   Establishing occupational status

Maintaining occupational status

Finding growing satisfaction in the occupation

Developing an avocation

Physical   Adjusting to physical slowdown

Adjusting to physiological changes in sex life

Social   Maintaining wholesome social relationships

Developing suitable leisure-time activities

Finding suitable diversionary interests

Evaluating and maintaining worthy motives for, and standards of, social conduct

Economic   Adjusting to the realization of maximum earning capacity

Establishing and maintaining adequate standard of living

Providing for educational expenses of children

Civic   Growing in civic interests

Accepting civic responsibilities

Spiritual Growth   Finding or maintaining a vital faith in Christ

Living consistently in keeping with a Christian philosophy of life

Maintaining meaningful personal and family worship

Growing in habitual use of the Bible as a spiritual guide

Making Christian witnessing a habit of life

Strengthening faith in theological truth

Church Relation	Maintaining a meaningful church relationship
	Assuming and discharging responsible places of service
	Establishing priorities in service activities
	Achieving one's place of greatest usefulness

SENIOR ADULTS

Family	Relating to grown children and in-laws
	Relating to grandchildren and great-grandchildren
	Adjusting to death of companion
	Accepting and adjusting to retirement-home situation
Vocational	Facing retirement realistically
	Adjusting to loss of occupation
	Finding new occupational pursuits
Physical	Accepting decreasing physical strength and health
	Accepting physiological changes in sex life
Social	Establishing explicit affiliation with the age group
	Finding leisure activities in keeping with strength

Developing new interests and social skills

Accepting declining social status

Economic
Adjusting to retirement income

Accepting a reduced economic standard of living

Civic
Continuing in concern for civic obligations

Discharging suitable civic responsibilities

Spiritual Growth
Finding increasing satisfaction in one's Christian faith

Maintaining a vital Christian view of life

Deriving growing satisfaction in worship

Finding the Bible as a source of comfort and inspiration

Maintaining fidelity to biblical truth

Church Relation
Maintaining a meaningful church relationship

Facing a declining role in active participation

Accepting a declining ability to serve

Adjusting to assumption of leadership roles by others

Surveying this projection of our adulthood, we may be struck by how incomplete our lives now appear in several respects. We may see ourselves as "heavy" in one respect and "lightweight" in another, thus initiating some fresh perception of any ego holes we have discovered to date.

Handling new experiences—even mentally—always exposes ego holes. How reassuring it is—what good news it is—that such holes are not weakness, although at this moment it is true enough that they are capable of causing us stress. Viewed properly, they actually represent opportunity and promise.

Thinking in terms of one's special blueprint, our ego holes are not holes at all, so much as vacancies or blank spots, parts of each internal design which as yet remain invisible because they have not yet received or responded to the call to development.

It is exciting to realize that as we learn to say *yes* to stress instead of denying the challenge, we each affirm our Self—God's unique design—with new boldness and power.

-6-

Stress From Physical Causes

When we encounter a period of unrelieved stress in our lives, the first thing to look for is some possible bodily cause. Jesus Christ gave us His perfect example for this, as time and again we read about His healing the physical person before He did anything at all about ministering to the sufferer spiritually.

God's Word says that my body is the temple of the Holy Spirit (*see* 1 Corinthians 6:19). When I consider that statement carefully I realize there is much more to it than first appears—that it implies real stewardship and responsibility on my part. God has placed me in authority over that temple, after all.

When did I last have a thorough physical checkup? Did it reveal any condition that needed treatment, and if so, did I follow through? And if I have any chronic ailment, do I maintain responsible, careful watch over it?

Subconscious worry about physical problems produces surprising quantities of stress and costs us untold amounts of emotional energy. On the other hand, the knowledge that we keep on top of our physical needs produces healthy feelings of self-esteem. The simple decision to maintain our bodies as God would have them kept will, for most of us, minimize more current stress than we realize.

The Cost of Indecision

A woman discovers a small lump in her breast which, as every woman should know, calls for immediate medical surveillance. The discovery throws her into a state of apprehension and fear. She feels she is "not up to" seeing her physician at this time, so pushes the unwelcome knowledge to the back of her mind.

The trouble is that she does not really forget it—not for one moment. Instead the vague but steadily increasing anxiety continually assaults her ego, creating a snowballing sort of inner distress all out of proportion to the facts. Should the lump prove cancerous, the woman is running a dangerous risk. If the tiny lesion is benign, as the majority are, what needless and costly pain she has allowed herself to suffer.

Incorrect Self-Diagnosis

An eighty-year-old woman became despondent and short-tempered, forgetful and moody, to the point at which her distracted family for the first time considered that it might be necessary to place her in a nursing home.

Fortunately the reason for her difficult behavior surfaced most unexpectedly one day during conversation with one of her elderly friends. "I've lived through a lot, but there's one thing I dread and can't stand to think of," she confided. "They're going to pull all my teeth."

The facts were that some weeks earlier the lady had discovered a tooth had loosened. She immediately assumed it would have to be extracted, and that then there would be no way to support her bridgework. There would be nothing else to do, she reasoned, but to extract her remaining teeth and fit her with dentures. From there she projected that if her lower teeth required pulling, surely the upper ones must be ready to go!

Her daughter, relieved to have overheard the conversation and to understand her mother's sudden symptoms of senility, rushed the dear soul to her dentist. The doctor recommended capping her lower teeth in order to strengthen them and improve them cosmetically. The procedure would be expensive, but the patient did not object. In fact, she sat straight up in the dentist's chair and shouted for joy!

Immediately a dramatic personality change took place. Not only did the aged lady's outlook improve, but her vanity reasserted itself. She began to "primp up" and drive out for shopping trips, visits, and bridge games. "I'll have to smile every day for the rest of my natural life, to get my money's worth out of these teeth," she says gaily.

A Realistic Look at Body Repairs

Some people react with great concern—even indignation—when something goes wrong with them physically. It's only realistic to expect our Selves to need repairs now and again, but certain individuals seem to find that fact nearly incomprehensible. Consequently, every day finds doctors seeing patients who have built up a full head of worry-steam long before making an appointment.

"Nobody should dread the possibilities of a medical diagnosis any longer than twenty-four hours," one doctor declared. That simple rule alone could preclude undue fretting for most of us. In that spirit, a husband who encountered several instances of sexual impotence did not waste time worrying about his "manhood" but consulted a urologist. The specialist found nothing organically wrong, and dismissed the patient with advice to let up on business pressures and take a short vacation.

"There's only one extraordinary aspect to this case," his doctor declared. "That is, my patient sought medical examination *first* instead of only as a last resort." Reassured by his physician, the man could accept his *temporary* impairment as just that—nothing more. He did not allow doubt and worry to augment the problem.

"Neurotic" or What?

It's surprising how often people may consult psychiatrists for some odd or unaccountable new pain or "funny feeling" they experience. Dr. Anthony Kowalski recounts having seen patients with chest pains being treated for neurotic problems, when they had histories of angina pectoris or myocardial infarction. The psychiatrist recalls:

Another woman who I saw, who had been treated for bloating of the stomach and peculiar pains in her shoulder, went on to having a gallstone the size of a large marble. Another condition which sometimes befuddles people is eustachiitis. In this condition the tube that goes from the back of the throat to the ear gets stopped up because of an infection, with the consequent effect that the air in the middle ear gets soaked up, creating a pressure on the middle ear mechanisms and causes dizziness and funny pains on the side of the head or in the neck. Unless one thinks of this condition, it is easy to define a person as having neurotic problems rather than a legitimate physical condition.

No one knows how often a primary source of emotional stress turns out to be some undetected physical malady: undiagnosed diabetes, for example, anemia, poor eyesight, heart palpitations, hypoglycemia, or a host of other possibilities.

Sometimes Christians tend to view stress difficulties as spiritual defects, instead of considering the possibility that some organic distress could be the culprit. The sincere Christian who prays to be delivered from her "migraine headaches and fatigue," believing that a visit to her doctor's office would indicate lack of faith, cannot discover—and be treated for—a brain tumor that actually exists.

I'm simply saying, *Let's don't try to diagnose our own cases.* See a doctor first. Let *him* rule out any possible physical reasons for your stress symptoms.

"There's Nothing Wrong With Me"

When Catherine and Bob met and married when both were in their late forties, they considered themselves supremely blessed of the Lord. After six months, however, their home atmosphere began to change. As Catherine became increasingly withdrawn, preoccupied, and fatigued, Bob became more and more concerned. "Honey, what's wrong?" he would ask, and the question invariably irritated her.

"I don't know. There are so many adjustments—I didn't expect housework to tire me like this—We seem to go, go, go all the time and never get any rest."

Bob began to see Catherine as someone quite different from the energetic and fun-loving woman he married. One day, as they attempted to discuss their situation, Catherine became defensive. "Maybe we should see a marriage counselor," she suggested.

"No, honey, I think you should see a doctor," Bob said.

"You know I'm healthy as a horse. I'm not due for my next physical exam for another six months. Anyhow, I know there's nothing wrong with me," she maintained.

Nevertheless, Bob persuaded her to see her doctor. The good man showed astonishment at his patient showing up six months early for her yearly physical, and as he examined her and found one test after another proving normal, they began to joke about it. "A waste of your time and my money," Catherine remarked—and just then the doctor discovered a tumor. The growth, already surprisingly large, needed to be removed without delay. Surgery was performed, the growth proved benign, and Catherine very soon returned to her upbeat attitudes and energetic life-style.

"If Bob had listened to me, if we had seen a marriage counselor instead of a doctor, we'd not have caught this problem early enough," Catherine confided. "My doctor said the tumor soon would have encroached on nearby organs. All sorts of complications could have developed. As it was, by finding it early, I had ideal conditions for surgery. Instead of illness or emergency surgery, I experienced health, happiness, and relief. The whole thing sure taught me a lesson."

Sleep and Stress

"Many times when people bring me long and complex recitations of their spiritual problems, I turn to them and ask a question that blows their minds: 'How long since you've had a full night's sleep?' " a minister said.

"Does that sound simplistic and noncaring? Well it isn't. You would be surprised how many people regularly cheat themselves of adequate sleep. Sleep deficiency can produce tremendous stress and even mental distortion," he added. "None of us can stay mentally or spiritually on the beam when we habitually burn the candle at both ends."

Workbook Assignment

Our bodies require three things for efficient operation: food, exercise, and sleep. List these categories on a workbook page entitled PHYSICAL CAUSES OF STRESS, leaving space for notes in each category.

We need to question ourselves about each of the three: Are we providing too much? Too little? A good balance? Comment on any which need changing. Note potential stress areas due to *excesses* (overweight—

Look sloppy? Feel heavy on my feet?) or *deficiencies* (too little exercise—Jogging? Tennis?) and so on.

Be as creative and as specific as possible when you consider areas needing change. Write down suggestions—Join exercise class. Go to bed one hour earlier each night. Also note the dates of your most recent physical examination and dental checkup.

Which suggestion on this page do you need to begin for yourself tomorrow? Write down your promise and place a date beside it. Congratulations!

-7-

Emotional Stress

"In my life, stress crowded in from all directions," Amy told me. "Like a snowball rolling downhill, it kept going faster, increasing in speed and in size as it hurtled along. In those days my life was filled with worry, fear, and anxiety. Everything seemed to be a matter of life or death. Though I considered myself to be a mature Christian, I wallowed in my problems instead of taking them to God.

"Problems consumed me; they dominated my thinking so I could not even converse at dinner. I couldn't do other things, like play golf or attend a party. I used to long to be able to go for a ride in the car with my husband and children and not worry about anything—just enjoy the ride."

Through the years Amy's problems had indeed snowballed, until she could no longer deal with them. For two years, however, she attempted to cope, attending Bible-study groups and prayer meetings in a desperate search for answers to her internal turmoil. Her friends loved her, exhorted her, prayed for her—and admonished Amy for her "lack of faith."

At last, however, Amy met someone who asked a new question: "Why don't you seek professional help?" After much prayer and thought Amy decided she wanted to do just that. She began to pray for help in finding a Christian psychiatrist, realizing that she needed someone who would approach her problems from a viewpoint consistent with the Scriptures.

"I saw I could not grow any more spiritually until I got help emotionally," Amy explained. "Yes, go to God; but also go to a counselor who knows how to help Him help you to sort out your problems."

Unresolved stress does indeed snowball. It takes courage and self-knowledge to recognize a need for psychological or psychiatric help to facilitate the healing which God wants us to experience.

After much hard work, Amy eventually emerged into fearless, exultant, healthy adulthood. In later chapters we will explore and utilize some of the effective ways in which she learned to deal with her complex of stress. With God's help we can go far in overcoming many stressful life situations. In some extraordinarily burdensome or complicated cases, however, the better part of wisdom is to recognize that we need professional help to facilitate our healing.

Possible Sources of Emotional Stress

What is the main source of my emotional stress? At first we may find ourselves unable to answer that question; it may take time and thought. Whole books are written on the subject of emotional stress, but here we can do little more than sketch in broad strokes some possible causes of the stresses we encounter. This chapter is meant to start you on your search for identifying your main stress sources.

Here are three main categories from which many of our problems may spring:

1. *Unrealistic expectations of myself* (my own or others')—Do I expect to work full-time, rear small children, and also maintain high cooking-and-housekeeping standards? What will happen to me emotionally? How will I begin to feel about myself? [Perhaps it should be noted here that although many of the stress situations used as examples appear to involve women primarily, the principles of stress situations—and how to handle them—apply for both men and women.]

2. *Abusive treatment*—Do I punish myself for falling short of my own impossible standards? Do I allow others to walk all over me? Do I work at a job where the boss erupts in torrents of contemptuous and abusive verbiage? Am I willing to "work myself to death"?

3. *Emotional deprivation*—Do I like myself? Do I allow others to express love for me? Is it possible for me to enjoy life's rewards and pleasures, or do I live in an atmosphere of emotional self-denial? Do I feel dull and lackluster, as though life is passing me by? Do I tell myself there is nothing to look forward to?

Perhaps at this point you do not know why you experience feelings of depression, worry, or fear. Perhaps you cannot isolate or name the stresses that beset you. In that case, don't try—for now. Leave your workbook page blank and return to it later. As we progress, you will achieve insights and understanding into the origins of feelings you presently cannot understand or cope with.

Dealing With Feelings

There is a way to deal with those feelings—a way that works, that can revolutionize your mental outlook, emotional health, and spiritual experience. We will learn how to distinguish between "inner stress" and "outer stress," deal with frustration, make strong decisions, increase our feelings of accomplishment and wholeness.

We can establish new self-concepts, learn ways to minimize the likelihood of failure, learn how to establish and revitalize relationships.

None of this will be easy, nor can it be accomplished without considerable work, thought, and prayer. The rewards are great, however, for it is as we begin to banish the baleful effects of emotional stress that we begin to understand and enjoy the abundant life which Jesus promised.

Principles of Overcoming Emotional Stress

The principles in this book will offer guidance, support, and a method for redirecting your life when stress attacks it. These principles represent a challenge to preparation. They can be studied, meditated upon, and practiced on during the smaller disturbances and interruptions all of us experience daily.

The ideas we will confront challenge us to begin in a fresh way the exciting discovery of our own resources —physical, psychological, spiritual—and to stimulate us individually to discover a life plan which allows us to respond holistically to our environment with deep satisfaction.

A Mental Picture of Our Goal

You might draw a simple diagram which will depict your goal, reproducing this in your workbook for future reference. It might go something like this:

Negatives	Positives
Failure	Success
Destructive	Constructive
Dull	Creative
Nervous	Confident

You get the idea. We want to build a bridge between any negatives that now exist in our emotional structure and the positives we intend to construct. Continue listing any other "building blocks" you can think of, making the list as personal as possible.

Will we do it? Can we actually accomplish what we have listed? Only as we are willing to return to that original blueprint, the Master Plan He designed, and will allow God to lovingly and patiently construct and remodel what He envisioned from before the very foundation of the world.

It will not be easy. It will not happen overnight. It will be comforting for us to realize, therefore, that our Father has plenty of time to devote to each of us.

- 8 -

Building Ego Strength

To return to Amy—her decision to consult a psychiatrist soon engendered some significant life changes which her friends rejoiced to see. Amy was the sort of person who brought everything she had to the task: intelligence and sensitivity, loving faith in the Lord, and a determination to cooperate fully with the doctor, who quickly earned her full respect.

The girl who had experienced so much emotional pain began to take small but consistent steps towards breaking free. "I used to stay on guard all the time, just waiting for the next thing to happen," she told me. "Now I can hardly wait to see what my doctor and I will accomplish next!"

One morning Amy telephoned to ask a favor. "Teddy, my doctor wants to explain exactly what my ego is and what we're trying to make it do. Would you come along and listen, then explain to me everything he says in words I can understand? I'm not sure I understand psychological terms, and this is one thing I must get right!"

We laughed about my "translating," but of course I

was pleased she asked me. At that moment I had no idea how valuable to me that meeting would become.

As the three of us sipped coffee in his office, Amy's doctor reached for paper and pencil and quickly sketched a "picture" of the ego and its functions, explaining and labeling as he went. (*See* next page.) I was fascinated—enthralled, in fact—as I recognized his genius in conveying to Amy and me some large truths in such graphic fashion. Not only could we grasp the concepts immediately, but I began to sense Amy's excitement as she understood for the first time some reasons for the welter of stress feelings she had endured for so many years.

Watching her eyes light up with interest, I knew what we must do. *The moment we leave,* I thought, *we're going home and draw that thing over and over until Amy gets totally thrilled that her ego is being strengthened right now!*

Engrossed in the doctor's ideas, Amy looked alive and at peace. *This hour is the beginning of something terribly good for my precious friend. Thank You, Jesus!,* I prayed silently. I felt so moved, so privileged to be part of it.

We stopped on our way home and bought a selection of colored pens. Then we sat at the kitchen table and drew, talked, shared, exchanged ideas, and praised God during an indescribably creative and unforgettable afternoon.

I want to share that EGO PICTURE with you, with the doctor's explanation of it following. Once we translate the somewhat complicated ideas into lay terminology,

EGO STRUCTURE

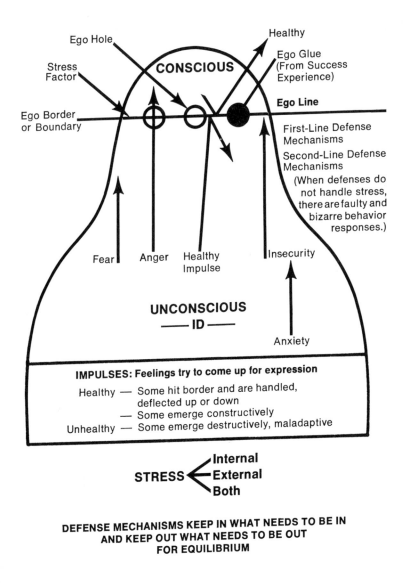

**DEFENSE MECHANISMS KEEP IN WHAT NEEDS TO BE IN
AND KEEP OUT WHAT NEEDS TO BE OUT
FOR EQUILIBRIUM**

we can understand (1) How the ego operates when it is healthy and (2) How it varies when it is disturbed.

Understanding these processes is Step One. Step Two, which we consider in the next chapter, is the simple, logical, and workable way to learn to strengthen an ego instead of weakening it, reinforce it instead of allowing it to stay under constant attack.

Amy and I named Step Two the "Key." It literally was to unlock doors for her so that God's healing light could shine into the darkest, scariest corners of her life. As the Key began with Amy that day, neither of us dreamed it might eventually be used of God to unlock many hundreds of other lives as well.

How the Ego Structure Works

A situation, expectation, or relationship exerts stress on the *ego line* (my level of awareness—that part of me which enables me to cope with life, stress, and so on).

Many times the ego line is in a weakened condition because of the presence of numerous *ego holes.* The ego holes developed on the ego line when first-line *defense mechanisms* continually proved inadequate to cope successfully with stress.

Example: A little child has a crisis experience which results in fear. He employs a good first-line defense mechanism: verbalization. As soon as the situation passes, however, his busy mother never really listens to him again or hears his true heart-cry of continued anxiety.

Often the child will then retreat to another defense mechanism (second-line) such as whining, clinging, hiding behind his mother. Every time certain new experiences which remind the child of the first crisis come along, and first-line defense mechanisms fail, the child begins to develop a pattern of second-line defense behavior unrelated to the specific stress situation.

The stress is too great for the ego line to handle. Thus up through the weakened spot (ego hole) comes the latent anxiety from his unconscious mind (still unresolved from earlier experiences). The individual then projects this feeling onto the present stress factor or onto other places or persons.

Problem: The child begins to develop a pattern of response by focusing the confusion and anxiety (emerging through his ego holes in a moment of stress) onto the person, object, or situation causing him stress at this moment. If this cannot be identified, he focuses it upon himself by internalizing it physically—as headaches, stomach aches and the like—or mentally or emotionally —as nervousness, sleeplessness, and so on.

Most often, however, he develops varying feelings of intense anxiety for the object, person, or situation which he "thinks" caused the present fear. He projects his fear, anxiety, anger, insecurity, or other feelings from the unconscious (and unresolved former experiences) onto the current situation, and may develop an aversion to it.

In this repeated behavior his level of awareness—his ability to interpret correctly—becomes distorted. If unhelped and continually submerged by unsuccessful attempts to cope, he will resort to more severe and bizarre second-line defense mechanisms which eventually may lead to "I give up."

Reconstructing Response to Stress

A person who lives with continual anxiety can learn to reconstruct his response to stress—to utilize first-line defense mechanisms and strengthen the ego line. As he is able to learn to reconstruct his responses to stress, he gradually will develop a more accurate level of awareness.

We conceptualize the results by envisioning success as producing *ego glue* with which we can fill up our ego holes. This strengthens the ego line and keeps the level of awareness within the boundary of reality.

Definition of Terms

Ego Line—Boundary where level of awareness rests most of the time.

Ego Holes—Disruptions or interruptions of the ego line, which allow unconscious material to enter awareness in various forms.

Defense Mechanisms—Neutral devices by which the mind maintains its equilibrium and stability.

First-Line Defense Mechanisms—Primary mechanisms. These are primarily psychological and initially are employed for stability and meeting stress.

Second-Line Defense Mechanisms—Used when first-line defense mechanisms weaken. These usually involve somatic or bodily reactions to stress.

Stress Factor—A stimulus from the internal or external world which tends to unbalance the mind's equilibrium set.

Ego Glue—Comprises externally and rationally motivated measures that aim to plug up the interruptions of the ego line and to support the weakened first-line defense mechanisms.

Conscious Mind—The "reporting" part of the nervous system of which we are *aware*.

Unconscious Mind—The "reporting" part of the nervous system of which we are *unaware*.

Amy Explains the "Ego Picture"

"My doctor is very practical and has so much common sense! He drew a diagram for me: first the ego line, and below that the subconscious, with holes formed when I was a child. I could keep stuff down in the holes, but adult stresses eventually would cause my subconscious material to rise and flow out of the ego holes. I was losing control of my feelings because stuff was coming up. I had too much stress for one person to take.

"Anxiety and nervousness are ego holes. We learned to plug those holes and get control of me. My ego then became strengthened.

"We developed new ways for me to respond to those stresses. Using the Key, I would work them out on paper. That kept me from getting confused and allowing my feelings to block out reality. The Key helped me gain control of my situation. It works every time."

-9-

Creative Response to Stress

Amy told me delightedly, "This year it seems I have fewer stresses, but that isn't true; I'm handling them before they can grow to any great size. I have begun to take control over my life to a great extent. There's much more joy. I don't have anxiety."

The Key unlocks a person's creative response to stress. Amy and I decided to name our stress-coping method the Key, because it is just that simple an instrument. Once she began using it faithfully, Amy testifies, the door of her life began to swing outward to a welcoming, rewarding world.

"Nowadays when I feel stress coming I anticipate that I'll handle it better this time than last time. In fact, it's almost funny. I rush to try the Key on every new stress that comes along, because I'm curious to see how it turns out," Amy said, laughing.

The Key Works for Everyone

Members of our family have shared this life-giving tool with all sorts of people: grammar-school children, politicians and other community leaders, clergymen, our housekeeper, teachers, strangers on airplanes.

No matter what size or shape a problem may be, the Key can help. We have used it time and again at home, during seminars, prayer groups, speeches to businessmen. Never has anyone told us, "The Key did not work for me."

The Heards use the Key so often that it almost has become a game. It has brought the varied stresses of a typically active household into manageable shape. It enhances the lives of one community-spirited judge and his car-pool-driving wife, not to mention the affairs of our son Larry, fifteen; daughter Teddy, thirteen; Susanna, eleven; and even our seven-year-old son, Denman.

How does it work? Easily. The Key, in fact, at first glance appears almost laughably simple. The formula is so short you can write it on an index card and keep it in your purse or pocket. When stress arises, you may use the Key in a matter of moments, or you might use it to work half a day at gaining deeply important new insights.

The Key to Solving Your Stress

There are four steps involved in using the Key in stress situations:

1. Identify the stress factor
2. Identify your feelings
3. Identify projection of feelings. (Uncontrolled responses to stress, second-line defenses on body?)

4. First-Line Defense Mechanisms
- Correct appraisal of situation
- Reevaluating goals and expectations
- Plan of action

That is virtually all there is to it. You will answer the same questions in the same order each time you deal with a stress situation. The range and complexity of the problems which produce stress are vast—yet in every case I have seen so far, the answer always comes out the same: the Key works!

Let's try a sample stress situation so you can observe the Key in action. After you use it one time, you should be able to utilize it well from then on—with immediate, encouraging, life-strengthening results. Chapter 10, "Ego Glue," will outline several situations where the Key has released troubled individuals from the paralysis and anxiety and tension and opened up a new world of God-given life potential. Here is how it worked for one man:

1. Identify the stress factor: A young doctor-in-residency has been assigned to the hospital emergency room.

2. Identify feelings: Fear, inadequacy, extreme anxiety.

3. Identify projection of feelings: Experienced waves of fear in his stomach, nausea, hyperventilation. These feelings, increasing as the weeks go by, make him wonder if he is too weak emotionally to stand the pressure of the responsibility.

4. First-Line Defense Mechanisms

• *Correct appraisal of situation:* He felt sure God had called him to a medical career. He felt he was in general well suited for medicine and he wanted to become a doctor.

• *Reevaluating goals and expectations:* The young doctor saw that simple lack of prior experience made him react emotionally to the sight of an ambulance arriving with some helpless victim. He realized that he had the potential ability to learn how to respond as a professional on the scene.

• *Plan of action:* Every night before going to sleep he would thank God for calling him to the medical profession. He would envision himself as he felt God wanted him to function in the emergency room, imagining himself relaxed, competent, caring. Each day as he arrived at the hospital he would consider the emergency room as a gymnasium for his soul. Every time a stretcher came in he would consider it an exercise against which this area of his inadequacy could respond in human experience. He recognized this *ego hole* as a place of unrealized potential in his life, an undeveloped area of his design which could develop into emotional strength.

RESULTS: As these concepts were practiced and became real in his life, he eventually felt gratitude for what he learned from the stress situations—a deep sense of calm confidence in the face of continued crisis.

Appraising Situations Correctly

Dr. Paul Tournier said, "The strong man is not he who hides his own failings from himself but he who knows them well."

Accordingly, we would do well to learn to recognize and listen to our voices of body, mind, emotions, and spirit, and to give equal time to each one. If our frustrations about not productively meeting a goal overshadow our abilities to think clearly while under pressure, we then cease to be creative in problem solving: we become our own enemies.

To appraise a situation correctly, we may have to ask ourselves numerous questions: What is the reality of the stress? What is necessary to handle it? (Here we must go beyond our instinctive reflexes.) *Who am I?*—in relation to the situation? *What do I want and need?* (Ask for a direct inspiration from God to answer this one.)

Sometimes one has to work hard at arriving at a clear view of a situation. To arrive at an honest appraisal, here are some questions to ask yourself:

How did this situation come about? At what place was my own identity threatened? What need does this situation represent for me? For others? At what time in the situation did I cease to act as God's agent? Do I experience myself functioning as God's agent at this time? Am I adding to the confusion of the situation? In what ways?

Questions About Ego Holes

To reevaluate ego holes, the following questions may prove helpful—ask yourself:

Is my present means of handling this stress a productive one? How? Is it unproductive? How?

What expectations of myself do I have in this situation? Are they realistic? What expectations of me do others have?

Is there any relationship in this situation which needs to be resolved? (Meditate on the relation of ego holes to that of unresolved conflict.)

How do I really feel in this relationship? Do my words accurately express my feelings? Do my actions accurately demonstrate my thoughts? Do I need to forgive someone? Do I need to ask someone to forgive me?

In some areas of my own life, I find I need to pass beyond my habit of automatic reflexive action to find even greater freedom. I realize that many decisions I make still result from unknown influences from my past, from prejudices, or from old goals I no longer value.

Reevaluating Expectations and Goals

Mother taught us, when we face a problem, always to ask: What does God want me to learn? How does God want to use me?

Accordingly, in order to change my response to the stress factor so I can be God's agent in the situation, I may have to change my unrealistic expectations of myself. Or I may have to refuse to respond to someone else's unrealistic expectations of me.

Verbal Action

One great source of power in the life of Jesus Christ came out of His congruity—His actions authentically demonstrated His words; His words authentically expressed His thoughts. He functioned as God's agent because of this consistently authentic expression of God's will and life as He related with men.

Question: Do I exhibit authentic consistency from *thought* to *word* to *action?*

-10-

Ego Glue

What in the world is ego glue? As Amy and so many of the rest of us are learning, ego glue is manufactured every time I respond creatively and correctly to stress situations. It fills in and mends my ego hole. Just as nature often mends broken bones so well that they actually become stronger at the fracture site, so do we literally help create in ourselves a new strength where once there was a hole.

Creative response to stress is something we can only learn through practice. As we apply the Key to one situation after another, it soon becomes almost automatic to do so—an unconscious strengthening reflex which averts many potential stresses before they can get to us. *We all need ego glue, because everybody has ego holes.*

Recording Progress

As we apply the Key to stress situations it is a good idea to record every step of the process in the notebook. (I shall want to refer to these transactions later.)

It is especially important to record *results* when we

use the Key, because they produce ego glue. As we read through some of our first small but important insights, it becomes obvious that God moves us very tenderly toward that unique blueprint He drew when first He envisioned each of us.

My own files contain many pages of Key transactions —mine, my family's, and those of friends. Each one is a love story, for it portrays in a beautiful way how much our Father loves us and longs to help us.

Some of these love stories follow. Reading them will show you how simply and effectively the Key can open some new doors in your own life. Far more importantly, however, these examples remind you that you belong to Him—and by His stripes you are healed.

Dealing With Impatient Father

1. Stress Factor: My father telephoned and angrily told me that I should have written my mother another letter; complained lengthily over my bad habit of not writing letters, my general thoughtlessness. He sounded furious with me.

2. Feelings (escaping through ego holes): Fear of my father; distress at having disappointed my mother; inadequacy over Daddy's considering me thoughtless and possessed of "bad habits."

3. Projection of Feelings Onto:

• *My own body*—While my father talked, I got a terrible, uneasy feeling in my stomach. I also felt as though my voice would not be as strong as I wished when I answered him.

- *My emotions*—I felt like a little child, completely inadequate and not knowing what to say. I felt terribly nervous.
- *My father*—I realized that I am afraid of him and do not always like to talk to him, because at some time in most of our conversations he becomes very critical of me. I kept wishing he would stop talking and hang up the phone.

4. **First-Line Defense Mechanisms**
- *Correct appraisal of situation:* I was not thoughtless, as I had already written a letter to Mother. I have difficulty in writing more often because I maintain a busy schedule. However, I write as often as I can. Ignoring correspondence is *not* a bad habit of mine. I did disappoint Mother because I don't write more often, and it makes my father angry that I don't write to her as often as he thinks I should. My anxiety resulted from fear of my father, as a consequence of former experiences in my childhood, rather than as a result of what he said about me.
- *Reevaluating goals* (if necessary): As far as writing, this is not necessary, for I honestly believe that I'm doing the best I can.
- *Plan of action* (honest verbalization):
  (a) Tell Daddy I am happy to write as often as I can, but my responsibilities do not permit me to spend a lot of time writing letters.
  (b) Tell Mother and Daddy that I am sorry if they think I am thoughtless and have this "bad habit," but I really do not think it is true.

(c) Realize that I am permitting my father to control my feelings and reactions—instead of Jesus Christ. I am "playing old tapes" from my childhood, when Daddy would get furious and I would have that frightened, inferior feeling. I am no longer that little child. I am an adult. Jesus is Lord of my life, and I ask Him to come be Lord of my feelings.

(d) Adult-to-adult conversation with my father whenever possible. As I am able, express to him verbally that a *correct appraisal of the situation* has been made, and that *reevaluation of goals* is unnecessary in this case.

"Just Plain Exhausted"

A young woman came to me for prayer. She said she was in great spiritual need and hoped to be delivered from her anxiety. She seemed distraught, appeared jittery, very tired and despairing. It took her two days to complete the Key. Later she gave me the following story in her own words:

1. Stress Factor: I accepted a job to help on the local symphony fund-raising team.

2. Feelings (escaping through ego holes): Growing anxiety, shaky feeling on the inside, extreme fear.

3. Projection of Feelings Onto:

   • *My body*—I am completely exhausted, worn out. I am too tired to do it. I am actually shaking when I think I have to do it.

- *My mind*—I am terrified that I must be losing my mind or having a nervous breakdown, if being a worker on the symphony drive upsets me this much. I am confused and don't know what to do— am dreading the first meeting. I must have serious spiritual problems and need prayer.

4. **First-Line Defense Mechanisms**

- *Correct appraisal of situation:* Teddy said to write down a list of all the "worlds" I live in, what my roles are, and what strengths are called for. FAMILY: Wife—partner, love, support. MOTHER: Patience, love, support. CHURCH: Teacher—initiate, respond, interpret. When I wrote down my whole list, I found that I was involved in thirteen different worlds, with a definite responsibility in nine of them. In seven of the nine roles a talent or strength is required of me which is not a natural, easy one for me—like teaching or speaking in front of people.

The thing I cannot stand to do is to go and ask someone for money. It embarrasses me, and I can't think of the right words to use. I never really know how to try to convince someone to give money.

I see now that my nervousness is not some unknown spiritual thing, but stems from too many roles—most of them requiring talents I don't have. I think I have gone beyond my tension-tolerance level and am just plain exhausted.

- *Reevaluating goals* (if necessary):
   (a) I don't have the stamina to do all these jobs.
   (b) One reason I agreed to do some of them was

to be with some of my friends. I don't have to work with my friends in order to be with them. Going out to lunch or going swimming would be easier and more fun.

(c) I should not commit myself to so many responsibilities that are difficult for me. Maybe I will go through my list and cut out some of the ones I really don't like doing.

(d) Include more fun things in my life. I think that I am too serious.

• *Plan of action* (honest verbalization, adult-to-adult):

(a) Telephone Joan and say that I'm sorry, but I made a mistake in accepting the job of working on the symphony team, and that I am already overcommitted timewise. If appropriate, mention that I really don't like to raise money, and since the main reason I accepted was so that we could do things together, ask her to bring Jenny and we will go swimming next week.

(b) Evaluate every single thing I am involved in. Make an honest decision about whether or not to continue doing it. Call and explain that I will not be able to continue in certain commitments.

RESULTS: I telephoned Joan and declined the symphony job. She said she knew how I felt because she felt the same way, but didn't know how to say *no* to the chairman. She asked me to join the team because she thought it would be fun for us to work together. I could hardly believe it—after feeling scared that she would think I was unreliable for begging off, after I had agreed to work. Now I really think she admires me for being honest. She accepted my invitation to go swimming. I really feel great. That felt so good—actually saying that I don't like to raise money!

SUCCESS EVALUATED: Increased ego glue, strengthened ego line.

Fear of Travel

A thirty-five-year-old woman phoned and confided that she literally had become ill over anticipation of an upcoming trip to Jamaica with her husband. She asked for prayer and said that she felt completely unable to make the trip unless she could be "delivered" from her aversion and inner pressure about it. We worked out the first part of the following outline, prayed together, and she completed the Key after returning from the trip. In her words:

1. **Stress Factor:** I am going on a trip to Jamaica. I am scared that I won't be able to sleep at night. I might lose control and start shaking. I am afraid that the couple we are traveling with will want to stay up late every night.

2. **Feelings** (escaping through ego holes): Scared, nervous, rushed, shaking, confused, filled with panic.

3. **Projection of feelings**
   - I have too much to do.

- I can't be ready for the trip on time and without wearing myself out.

4. **First-Line Defense Mechanisms**

- *Correct appraisal of situation*

    (a) I can take a sleeping pill to ease any insomnia.

    (b) Nothing will make me lose control. We will be sleeping late, taking naps, playing golf, swimming, and eating good food. I will be with my husband the whole time and can experience security.

    (c) If our friends want to stay up late, there will be other couples in the hotel who can join them. We also have other friends in Jamaica who can entertain them.

- *Reevaluating goals* (if necessary): Instead of being the life-of-the-party type, I am a slightly tired mother who needs a vacation which will allow me to "do my own thing," even if it is just sleeping late.

- *Plan of action* (honest verbalization, adult-to-adult): Write or phone our friends and tell them that we are going to Jamaica for rest and sleep as well as fun, and we hope they will understand.

RESULTS: Ego glue. My week of complete relaxation, exercise, and delicious meals gave me a real lift. After using the Key, I felt relaxed, happy, self-confident, and in control of the situation. I left for Jamaica expecting to enjoy a delightful vacation—and did!

Anxiety Over New Job

A forty-year-old woman embarked on a part-time job shortly after her release from a mental institution. She suffered an onslaught of fear and anxiety about her ability to do the work. I showed her how to use the Key, and she relates the results:

1. **Stress Factor:** Last week was my first week on a new job. I had not worked in fifteen years. My first day at the office I was very nervous. My nervousness increased when I saw my employer bring in a typewriter for me to use, as I am a very slow typist and had been out of practice for some time.

2. **Feelings:** For the first couple of hours I was occupied with some simple work my employer gave me to do. As I worked I felt my nervousness subside and I became calmer.

3. **Projection of Feelings:** Then my employer brought up the matter of typing some letters. I envisioned myself at the typewriter—pick and peck, very slowly, as my employer watched, and I made many mistakes. To add to this, I had noticed another secretary earlier, typing very rapidly. Other people in the office appeared competent and able, and my nervousness and anxiety grew into fear as I realized that I could never get the typing done while others watched me.

4. **First-Line Defense Mechanisms**
   - *Correct appraisal of situation:* What was I to do? My job is from nine o'clock until noon each day. I only had one hour left, with three letters due

the next day. I couldn't stay late because I had an appointment with my psychiatrist. As I turned all this over in my mind, I determined to tell my employer I would do the typing at home and bring it in the next day. At home I could work alone, with no one watching, and with no time pressure. When I suggested this to my employer, she had no objections.

• *Reevaluating goals* (if necessary): That afternoon I discussed my situation with my doctor. He felt I could do the work, since I had all evening free. He suggested that I begin typing lessons.

• *Plan of action:* Feeling much relief, I went home and began my work. As I completed each page without mistakes, unhurried and free from interruptions, I felt my confidence returning and felt satisfaction at my accomplishment. The nervousness and feelings of fear vanished. I returned to the office the next morning, calm and at ease, confident that with continued practice through my beginning typing lessons I could handle the work at my new job.

RESULTS: Ego glue. Strengthened self-esteem.

Ordeal of the Panicky Party-Giver

The Key helped another woman learn to organize her time and talents successfully so that she could handle her social obligations and enjoy them. As she tells it:

1. **Stress Factor:** My husband and I could no longer afford to hire housekeeping help. Never in my life had

I cooked anything but scrambled eggs or fudge, and now I had to prepare three meals a day, carry laundry to the laundromat, clean house, and run errands.

2. **Feelings:** At first it all seemed an enormous ordeal for me. Eventually, after I became fairly successful at housekeeping, we ventured into entertaining one or two couples for dinner. After getting the house ready, polishing silver, setting the table, arranging flowers, and getting myself dressed and prepared to receive guests, I felt panicky.

3. **Projection of Feelings:** Minimal

4. **First-Line Defense Mechanisms**

- *Correct appraisal of situation:* I realized that I must learn to reorganize my time and whatever talents I had.

- *Reevaluating goals* (not necessary).

- *Plan of action:* I bought several cookbooks and began to collect recipes for do-ahead dishes such as hors d'oeuvres which could be prepared early and frozen until needed. I tried to find unusual foods that not only would please our guests, but my husband as well.

When my husband asked to invite twenty people for a dinner party, I panicked again. However, I realized that by preparing ahead of time I could manage. My husband served the juices and appetizers. The only time I had to be away from my guests was for about fifteen minutes—to reheat the hors d'oeuvres and two vegetables.

When our guests returned for second servings, I realized that the party was a success and that I could easily repeat that success by advance planning. We have given a number of parties since then. Except for my husband's help in serving, I have learned to manage by myself.

RESULTS: Ego glue. New tasks were successfully completed. "Our parties have been successful and a lot of fun!"

The Death Wish

A seventy-nine-year-old woman had "a very happy childhood and loved life, people, dancing, parties, and made excellent grades in school." She married her childhood sweetheart, a man of integrity and honesty. He loved her, and she returned his love. Increasing years brought problems, as her use of the Key reveals:

1. **Stress Factor:** When I reached age seventy, I began to have many problems, the principal one being my husband's health. Also, I had to have several major but not critical operations.

About six years ago my husband became completely helpless physically and began having mental problems of senility. At his request, I kept him in our home those next four years, with nurses around the clock. Eventually I saw that I could no longer do for him at home the things a hospital could do to make him comfortable.

During that time my son lost his beautiful thirty-eight-year-old wife to cancer, leaving four little boys from eight to fifteen years of age. My brother died five weeks later. My daughter was in a psychiatric hospital.

I had to have surgery on both eyes and was in the

hospital for four weeks with influenza. I began suffering great pain from arthritis of the spine, and then discovered a diabetic condition which affects the movement of my lower extremities.

2. **Feelings:** Uselessness, depression.

3. **Projection of Feelings:** For the first time in my life, at age seventy-four, I entered into deep depression. It never occurred to me to take my own life, but I would wake up at night wishing that I could go to sleep and not wake up, since I could no longer be useful to my children and grandchildren.

4. **First-Line Defense Mechanisms**

- *Correct appraisal of situation:* After a period of time, I knew that my death, even though I wished it, would be a burden and loss to my children. I realized that there were other ways of helping them than by being *physically* useful.

- *Reevaluating goals* (not necessary).

- *Plan of action:* With daily prayer to God, and with the knowledge that He hears, He has lifted me out of my desire for death. I still get discouraged sometimes that I can't do many things physically to help my family, but they show me in many affectionate ways that they return my love. I pray constantly for the welfare of each one of our wonderful family.

RESULTS: Ego glue. Believing in the efficacy of prayer, this devoted grandmother realized that daily prayer for loved ones is as important—vital, in fact—as any act of physical devotion.

- II -

Love Power

Karl Barth, the theologian, when asked to sum up his religious beliefs in one sentence, said: "Jesus loves me."

That is true—and it is a great mystery. Never will we understand love, but each of us—even the most desperately deprived—knows love exists, and we cry out to someone, anyone, to speak to that terrible need.

Once Wyatt and I conducted a seminar entitled "Creative Response to Stress," and we invited the group of young single people to practice using the Key.

A young man nobody knew had wandered in off the street and found his way into our midst. Dirty, shabby, unkempt, he kept saying he did not belong there and ought to leave. Of course we encouraged him to remain, but when Wyatt passed paper and pencils around and invited everyone to try the Key, our new friend Gilbert hardly seemed to bother.

When the seminar ended, Wyatt and I were pleased to see our perceptive and caring young churchmen surround Gilbert and invite him to join them at the ice-cream shop. Wyatt walked over to the light switch, then stooped to pick up a paper from the floor. It was

Gilbert's attempt at working the Key. We stood reading it through tears, for this was a classic document of *lost* ness:

My name is Gilbert. After I spent six years in Gatesville State School for Boys, I haven't been able to make something out of myself. I been in San Antonio State Hospital three times and I still can't make it.

I'm on probation for 5 years. And I'd already violated three times. Next time there won't be another chance. I need church, more understanding and love. I want to straighten up and fly right. Look for job and try to be somebody. I'm serious. Thank you.

FRIEND

This is only the second time I been to church. I need more.

I.   Identify stress factor
   A. I'm scared I won't make my probation.
   B. Don't want to go to the pen.
II. Identify feelings
   A. Mad and worried.
   B. I need help and a job.
I'm on probation! I'm scared I'll steal!

A Matter of Life and Death

Never will Wyatt and I be able to forget Gilbert and his heart-cry. Too inarticulate to put the information into spoken words, too despair-ridden to attempt to relate to others, Gilbert—yes, and all his brothers in this broken world—cries out for the one thing that can save his life. *Love.*

Dear God, will I answer that unspoken cry? Do I truly understand it is a matter of life and death?

God Loves Me

The Bible says, "If God be for us, who can be against us?" (*see* Romans 8:31). A psychologist puts it this way: "The way self-esteem and security come together has much to do with how we think about ourself, and self-opinion has much to do with ego."

Jesus loves me, but can I love myself? Can I like myself? Forgive myself?

"If you like yourself and feel secure, and if you can respond to and meet constructively the stress challenges that threaten your ego, you will become an independent, responsible, and mature person who is able to love, integrate and actualize into a Christian nature," the psychologist observed.

On the other hand, if we experience repeated failure, with no "successes" to alleviate our feelings, we can get very down on ourselves and develop weak ego patterns. That makes us unable to make decisions from a standpoint of faith, optimism, and other healthy personality traits. Instead, we operate out of fear, anxiety, and worry.

I Can Learn to Love Me

As use of the Key enables ego glue to pour into my unwelcome ego holes, something exciting can happen to me. My self-concept begins to change, and as that happens, as my focus shifts from preoccupation with my own stress-filled life to a new concern for others, my life can begin to grow.

That's *Love Power!*

Love is the *current* on which our responses travel. Love is the *power* which orders life and generates growth. Love is the *energy* by which an ego functions, by which it is convicted in its lethargy, motivated at its resource level, and continually stimulated to produce joy through appropriate life responses.

I Can Learn to Love You

Love Power makes it possible for me to deal with broken relationships. I can learn to love you, just as you are, and despite my own deficiencies.

When I lose my community of support, I feel detached, isolated, and I have no roots. When my ego becomes sound enough to permit me to run the risk of loving, however, I enter into a community. Here I discover that the love of Jesus Christ brings immediate security, for I know I am forgiven, and the guilt factor is taken away.

I can learn to love you, and I learn also that love generates more love. And if I get into a Christian church, I begin to get my relationships onto a sound basis. Wyatt and I visited a home recently where God has done a marvelous work. "We have Christian friends we never knew before," the husband told us.

In this milieu of relationships the couple found themselves and saved their floundering marriage—because when they found them*selves* they found each other. That's Love Power!

Is Love a Reality in My Life?

I need Love Power to provide the five elements within any close relationship: empathy, respect, honesty, concreteness in communication, willingness to confront another.

In my relationships, Love Power enables me to:

- Meet you at the level that you come to me.
- Be a bearer of God's love for you in whatever physical environment is necessary.
- Continue to appreciate myself and approve my motives in our relationship regardless of the reactions of others.

Once my mother told me about JOY: J—Jesus first; O—Others second; Y—Yourself last. That's Love Power!

Six Powerful Ways Love Responds to Stress

1. Love yearns to make complete that which is incomplete.

2. Love yearns to put together that which has fallen apart or has shattered.

3. Love yearns to make whole.

4. Love yearns to experience union with the object of its desire—to supplement, to strengthen, and to become part of, or to be supplemented, strengthened, or completed.

5. Love is the glue which holds together our ego structure (mental and emotional level of awareness and coping abilities), that we might correctly interpret life and respond creatively and successfully to it.

6. Love brings to life that fluid integration in which we move, live well, and have our being.

Jesus Loves Me

That truth suffices—it stands up to anything this life can throw at us. The Bible says, "I can do all things through Christ which strengtheneth me" (Philippians 4:13).

Scripture records an incredible list of tribulations suffered by the Apostle Paul: hunger, cold, nakedness, beatings, imprisonment, shipwreck, homelessness, physical abuse. How did Paul respond to stress? In his powerful Letter to the Romans, Paul challenges me to the depths of my being:

Who shall separate us from the love of Christ? shall tribulation, or distress, or persecution, or famine, or nakedness, or peril, or sword?

As it is written, For thy sake we are killed all the day long; we are accounted as sheep for the slaughter.

Nay, in all these things we are more than conquerors through him that loved us.

For I am persuaded, that neither death, nor life, nor angels, nor principalities, nor powers, nor things present, nor things to come,

Nor height, nor depth, nor any other creature, shall be able to separate us from the love of God, which is in Christ Jesus our Lord.

Romans 8:35–39

-12-

The Language of Love

Every love relationship has a language.

How do I learn who *you* are? Do you tell me with your words? Your life-style? The way you smile at me, or simply touch my hand?

In Jesus, God demonstrated the power of perfect communication. His words, thoughts, and actions matched and were congruent. No wonder that God's Son communicated with such power. "Follow Me," He said, and the Bible tells us they laid down their nets and followed Him.

Communication is one urgent goal of love. We yearn to communicate because we need to communicate. We reach out and touch one another with a word, a smile, or even silence. The language of love includes rich, long silences at times, and it also knows how to listen.

Love Letter to You, My Friend
Did you ever have such a funny friend—one who loves to get a new, fat, yellow legal pad and write great, long letters?

My letters are so filled up with my soul, as I try with

all that is in me to make myself heard and understood by another one of God's persons, who, according to how I hear and experience him, speaks my language. I confess I never have thought for a moment that my insight might be incorrect. The question is how to make the communication in such a way that my word accurately conveys my thoughts and desire to be your friend.

There really is only one way, and that is to embody the thoughts and words in action. When we see the people we love often—and unite our lives in common goals and aspirations—our love can grow as the relationship deepens: the whole experience can be productive.

But when people cannot be together and the expression of mind and soul comes by word, the word can only be believed by faith—for there is no corresponding visible action to demonstrate that "your word is truth."

God's Love Language

I cannot express to you the tears of new understanding of our dear Heavenly Father which I have shed today. A clear revelation came to me of how God in the flesh sought a way to make communication with us: a way that would *demonstrate* that His Word *accurately* conveyed His thoughts and His desire to be our Friend.

The big question is: How can I communicate my love to another so my *words* accurately convey my thoughts? Do my actions accurately demonstrate my words?

Thoughts → Words → Actions

Is there an accurate transmission of Thought → Word

→ Action? Is this essential to an accurate interpretation? What can I do if my thought transmission becomes misinterpreted? Especially by someone I love?

God's Word tells us to *speak the truth in love*. What a divine lesson in communication! Especially since I am seeing how hard it is to *speak*, how difficult to *know the truth* and—sometimes, at least—how almost impossible to *love*.

Sending Heart Messages

There is a language of the heart. We need to learn how to send our heart messages more accurately and to learn how to discern another's heart messages more perceptively.

How can I accurately communicate the following ideas to you so that you would understand me clearly? (Perhaps you would like to include this exercise in your workbook.)

			Expectations
Thoughts	Words	Actions	Reactions
I like you.			
I need you.			
I want to work with you.			
You challenge me.			
You make me feel good.			
You need me.			
What I have to offer you will benefit you.			

I am not going anyplace.
I want to learn about
   you.
I want my relationships
   to be life-giving and
   in the light.
I want to receive from
   you.

To Speak the Truth in Love

When we were first married, I did not always express my desires verbally when they differed from Wyatt's, especially when it did not matter too much to me at the time. I thought I was being thoughtful in doing this, and in the Name of Christ was being a good, submissive wife. This became a pattern of behavior for me in our relationship, though neither of us realized the significance of what I was doing.

Years later, I happened to accompany Wyatt to the Executive Businessmen's Seminar at Dr. Clyde Narramore's Narramore Christian Foundation, for which Wyatt serves as a trustee. During our visit, Dr. Wayne Colwell helped me understand for the first time that when I do not use my words to authentically express my feelings I actually do Wyatt an injustice.

By not verbalizing my desires, I am failing to give him adequate information so that we can make decisions which represent the interests and desires of *both* of us. And if I have not shared my information with him, Wyatt cannot include my best interests when he makes decisions on behalf of us.

Good communication does not come easily, nor is it cheap. It costs us some effort, some risk of rejection, some misunderstandings. But God calls us to make that effort. Christ says, "Love one another." I must practice to make myself more nearly perfect in love, and in God's language of love. It is important to Him.

An Exercise

Choose a person who is close to you. Identify a heart message you have for that person. How would you transmit that thought in words? In actions?

Example: How can I convey, "You are precious to me"?

-13-

Redirecting Your Life

A letter on my desk asks a challenging question: "Teddy, what one thing could I do that would really ignite my life?"

What a marvelous, stimulating thought! I turn it over and over in my mind, and at last decide on a one-word answer: "Commit."

"Now just exactly what does *that* mean?" I can hear my friend asking, and I have to answer her in words something like this: "Beloved, I really don't know *exactly.* I believe you are yearning to go deeper into life, but nobody but God and you know where you are at any given moment. *Commit yourself.* Offer to let God use you today. Start giving yourself away, and see what God wants to give you in return."

If you are serious about wanting to ignite your life, let me share with you two thoughts from the great psychiatrist Carl Jung in his book *Memories, Dreams, Reflections.* He commented on two phases of life that are life-changing, if taken seriously. First he attempted to understand the dark side of his life: "When something emotionally vulgar or banal came up, I would say to myself, it is perfectly true that I have thought and felt this way at some time or other, but I don't have to think and feel that way now. I need not accept this banality of mine in perpetuity; that is an unnecessary humiliation."

The Apostle Paul had substantially the same discussion with himself when he wrote the seventh chapter of the Book of Romans. Read this chapter and see what solution Paul found for the dilemma that is within us all.

The second phase discussed by Dr. Jung dealt with the difference between thought processes and action. He said there was "a tremendous difference between intending to tell something and actually telling it. In order to be as honest as possible with myself, I wrote everything down very carefully, following the old Greek maxim: 'Give away all that thou hast, then shalt thou receive.'" What was it that Christ said?—"If any man desire to be first, the same shall be last of all, and servant of all" (*see* Mark 9:35).

Igniting life is scary and even risky sometimes. But it is only when we are willing to change and grow that we touch life where it is green. Touching the dead bark on the outside of life has few risks—likewise it has the fewest rewards.

Some Life-Changing Ideas

For any of you who need some more specific suggestions, here is a list of ideas which are almost sure to be life-igniting:

1. Memorize Scripture. You empower your life when you begin to hide God's Word in your heart. You can

memorize Scripture one verse at a time, during your quiet time, while bathing, washing dishes, driving your car, and so on.

2. Obtain and read a Bible which has notes on how to present the Gospel of Jesus Christ to another person. Helping someone relate to the Gospel in his or her life is indeed a high calling, and being a facilitator—as someone makes a personal commitment to Christ—is the *name of the game.*

3. If you are having a difficult time just now, read and reread the following Scripture, supplying your own name for "the world."

> For God so loved the world, that he gave his only begotten Son, that whosoever believeth in him should not perish, but have everlasting life.
>
> John 3:16

4. Read Psalms 91 every night before you go to sleep.

5. Each morning pray something like this: *Dear God, I give myself to You for today. Please come live this day with me. Praise Your Name. Amen.*

Other New Directions

As we strengthen our psychological resources, it helps to take inventory at times, if only to see how far God has brought us—and to praise His Holy Name.

The following principles absolutely provide new ego glue as you use them. It is a good idea to decide to practice these consciously, even on a one-a-day basis, until ego-strengthening habits grab hold. Use the Key regularly.

1. Do what you *know* is right. If you are not yet certain what to do, talk to someone whose opinion you respect. You do not need to know that person well; it is more important that you know that you are getting objective counseling.

2. Take the initiative in restoring a broken relationship on the same day the break occurs. Even when you do not understand or feel responsible, you can say something like, "I want to tell you that I am sorry for whatever part I played in this misunderstanding." Immediately, in the same conversation if possible, do your part, no matter how difficult it may be for you, in building a bridge. Then just remain quietly receptive as the other person works out his or her situation.

3. If someone criticizes you unjustly, say, "I am glad you feel free enough in our relationship to express your opinion. I have another feeling which seems more valid for me."

If someone criticizes you with inaccurate information, say, "I am glad you feel free to express your feelings, but the information I have is different from what you have shared."

When it is possible and truthful, agree with someone who makes a derogatory comment about you.

The above principles are just "starters." As you discover new, workable ways to affirm your "I am," you will want to write them down and put them into practice.

Perhaps you need a new springboard for your faith—
some different ways in which you can challenge and
redirect your thinking as a Christian. The following
"seminar" can be used very effectively by you alone,
but I believe you will enjoy it tremendously when you
gather a group of "seekers" for an evening of discussion.

1. At what time in my life was God the most real to
me?

2. What is the most vivid prayer experience I ever
had?

3. What is my greatest need today? Think of the
strength that would enable you to meet that need. Read
First Corinthians. Claim the strength.

Discussion Group: Read John 4:5–32

1. What is the single most impressive point to you
personally of this story, "The Woman at the Well"?

2. What need in your own life could be met by *applying* your answer to the first question?

3. In which specific places or with which persons do
you have the greatest difficulty sharing your faith?
Where do you feel uncomfortable? Verbally? With your
life?

4. Have you developed a value system as a Christian
which says there are some places you will not go or
some people you will not associate with? Where did you
get this idea?

5. Why do you think it did not seem to bother Jesus
where He was or who He was with? (*Note:* He had a

purpose and He knew His identity.)

6. From where do you receive your identity? Whose opinions do you allow to control your actions, feelings?

God's Word in Me: His Promise

> For as the rain cometh down, and the snow from heaven, and returneth not thither, but watereth the earth, and maketh it bring forth and bud, that it may give seed to the sower and bread to the eater: So shall my word be that goeth forth out of my mouth: it shall not return unto me void, but it shall accomplish that which I please, and it shall prosper in the thing whereto I sent it.

> Isaiah 55:10,11

1. As God shows you a part of His Word that you feel He would like you to experience as your own response, underline it in your Bible.

2. At the top of a page in your notebook, put a word to describe it: JOY, POWER, and so on. I discover these parts of the Word best when I recognize a need. For example, if I am discouraged, maybe He shows me that what He would like to give me is His strength or His confidence. Thus, at the top of my page, I would first write: STRENGTH. Under that, write: MY NEED—I AM DISCOURAGED. Date it.

3. Then get your concordance and look up "strength." Underline the verses in your Bible and write them down in your notebook.

4. As you write the verses in your book, pray, "Oh,

God, as I write Your Word in this book, so may Christ's Spirit write it in the fiber of my life."

5. Through the day, rather than thinking, *I am going to be filled with joy, I am going to be strong,* or *I need the gift of healing,* pray: "Father, thank You for Your Word. I open to You the area of my life where You have shown me a need." (Here mention discouraged attitude, inability to help a friend who is sick, anger—or whatever your specific need.) Then, for example:

Father, You have brought to my attention Your Word in this area of anger. ["Be ye angry, and sin not: let not the sun go down upon your wrath" (Ephesians 4:26).] I ask now that You give me the courage to allow Your Word to be my response in this misunderstanding. I plan to go and say that I am sorry for whatever part in the misunderstanding is mine, before the day passes.

Or in another case:

Father, I have opened my life to the full entry of Your Spirit. I simply ask the Holy Spirit to be free in me to incarnate Christ's power as He needs me to be a channel of His love. I pray for the release of Your indwelling Word. I yearn to be a temple of Your love for the glory of Christ. I praise You and affirm to You Your freedom in me to incarnate and make alive in my flesh Your own life, Your fruit, Your gifts as You choose. ***Praise the Majestic Lord of all lords and King of all kings!***

6. Wait and watch and be at work *loving.* Be expectant and at His choosing, and you soon will shout with a joyful noise, "Praise the Lord, He has called forth His Word from my life for His glory, as a demonstration of union with Him and as an experience whereby I may know Him in Spirit and in Truth."

So do we redirect our lives. If you do these things your little book will grow, *you* will grow, and you will see beautiful things emerging as God's Word becomes creative in you and through you in those you love.

Commit yourself. With God's help, using the Key, seek your own creative response to stress. He will help you overcome the world, even as He completes His own divine design for your unique Self. *Love* and *power* to you!

Hold High the Torch

Hold high the torch!
You did not light its glow—
'Twas given you by other hands, you know.
'Tis yours to keep it burning bright,
Yours to pass on when you no more need light;
For there are other feet that we must guide,
And other forms go marching by our side;
Their eyes are watching every smile and tear
And efforts which we think are not worthwhile,
Are sometimes just the very helps they need,
Actions to which their souls would give most heed;
So that in turn they'll hold it high
And say, "I watched someone else carry it this way."
If brighter paths should beckon you to choose,
Would your small gain compare with all you'd lose?
Hold high the torch!
You did not light its glow—
'Twas given you by other hands, you know.
I think it started down the pathway bright,
The day the Maker said: "Let there be light."
And He once said, who hung on Calvary's tree—
"Ye are the light of the world." . . . Go! . . . Shine—
    for me.

ANONYMOUS

Epilogue

Teddy Moody Heard was a beautiful, vivacious mother of four children—and my wife. She went into the hospital on February 7, 1974, for a routine hysterectomy from which she never recovered. Until her untimely death on March 4, 1974, she had had remarkable impact upon the lives of hundreds of people and possessed a wisdom far beyond her years. In the latter part of her life she became more free, more open in the manner in which she encountered other people at a deep level. Hence this book.

It was not completely finished at the time of her death, and therefore, as her husband, it became necessary for me to finish the book as a legacy to her children, Larry, Teddy, Susanna, and Denman. I have attempted to make the words *her* words, the thoughts *her* thoughts, the feelings contained in the book *her* feelings. It is never easy to finish a project commenced by someone else, but I have attempted to be true to what I felt she was endeavoring to express in the latter years of her life. Her Christian witness was profound, and she had a high visibility in church leadership in Houston and far beyond. She began her unique ministry from the podium, but her personality grew and developed as she encountered and interacted with other people in small, sharing groups. The result was that she became even more open. She said, "To encounter people *where they are* with the love of Jesus Christ is quality time, and that is *where it is."*

Part of the book was mine, because we spent many hours discussing and rehashing it, but the guiding genius of this book is the result of the devoted Christian life of a woman who understood the Christian message at its most common denominator—"within"—and she developed techniques of sharing the intimacy of Christ with other people in a most profound way.

Wyatt H. Heard
Houston, Texas